CASH, CREDIT, AND YOUR FINANCES: THE TEEN YEARS

BY JILL RUSSO FOSTER

Copyright © 2009 Jill Russo Foster

ISBN: 978-0-9817557-1-7

Library of Congress Cataloging & Publication Data
Foster, Jill Russo
Cash, Credit and Your Finances: The Teen Years
Registration # TX0006895246 / 2008-06-06

All rights reserved, including the right to reproduce this book or portion thereof in any form whatsoever.

Printed in the USA

To my husband Dave, for all of your support and encouragement.

To my father Tony, with thanks for being there for me.

To the people who helped make my ideas about this book a reality: Deirdre Silberstein of Silberstein & Associates LLC, Kim Barron of New Leaf Design, ChaChanna Simpson of Twentity.com, and Barbara Garelick of BGE Print.

Thank you, all.

DISCLAIMER

This book is for information purposes only. It is not meant to be legal, tax, and/or financial advice and should NOT be relied upon or treated as legal, tax, and/or financial advice. Please consult your financial and/or legal advisors for specific information regarding your personal circumstances.

TABLE OF CONTENTS

INTRODUCTION 1

CHAPTER 1: BASIC CONCEPTS PERSONAL FINANCE 5

    MANAGING YOUR MONEY 5

    TOOLS FOR MANAGING YOUR MONEY 6

    BUDGETING 7

    FINANCIAL RECORDKEEPING 11

    TAXES 14

    SAVINGS 16

    HANDLING YOUR ALLOWANCE 18

    HANDLING YOUR FIRST PAYCHECK 20

    PREVENTING IDENTITY THEFT 22

CHAPTER 2: WORKING WITH A BANK 27

    THE BANKING SYSTEM 27

        Types of Banks 28

        Types of Bank Accounts 32

        Bank Services 36

        Bank Fees and Charges 38

        Choosing a Bank 40

    OPENING AND WORKING WITH BANK ACCOUNTS 41

        How to Open a Bank Account 41

Balancing a Checking Account 47
ELECTRONIC BANKING 48

CHAPTER 3: CREDIT AND DEBT 53
ESTABLISHING CREDIT 53
CREDIT CARDS 55
    Credit Card Fees and Terms 59
    Using Your Credit Card Wisely 60
MANAGING CREDIT 62
    Your Credit Report 62
    Your Credit Score 64
MANAGING DEBT 66
BORROWING FROM OR LENDING TO A FRIEND 68

CHAPTER 4: PAYING FOR YOUR EDUCATION 71
STRATEGIES FOR PAYING FOR YOUR EDUCATION ..72
    Savings 73
    Scholarships 74
    Loans 74
    Financial Aid 76
    Work/Study Programs 76
TYPES OF STUDENT LOANS AND FINANCIAL AID
    PACKAGES 77
    Federal Government Programs 77
    State Government Programs 78

School Programs 81
Private Programs 81
STANDARD TERMS OF LOAN PACKAGES 83
HOW TO APPLY FOR SCHOLARSHIPS, STUDENT LOANS AND FINANCIAL AID PACKAGES 84
   Qualifying for Scholarships, Loans, and Financial Aid 84
   Applying for Scholarships and Financial Aid 85
   Applying for Federal Government Student Loan Packages 85
   Applying for Loans from Financial Lenders 86
   Applying for Scholarships or Grants from Other Entities 86
PAYING BACK YOUR LOANS 87

CHAPTER 5: MAJOR PURCHASES 89
ABOUT CONTRACTS 89
MAKING PURCHASES 91
   Purchasing Telephone and Internet Services 92
   Purchasing High Technology Products 96
   Purchasing Your Own Car 98
   Purchasing Over the Internet 100
WARRANTIES 102
INSURANCE 104

AFTERWORD: WHAT THE TEENAGERS LEARNED 109

GLOSSARY **111**
INDEX **117**

INTRODUCTION

I've always been amazed at how people – including me – handle their money. I started my career in the financial world as a bank teller right out of college. I was working in an affluent area, and many of my customers wore designer clothes and drove prestigious cars. But many of them were also on the overdraft list. How were they living?

During this same period, I wanted to establish my own credit, so I made a game out of how many credit cards I could get. My high was 27 cards! It took me many years to pay off the balances I accumulated.

I now work in the mortgage industry, and I see people who are seriously in debt or who have little or no savings. They need to refinance their homes to use the equity to pay off their consumer debt. And then they come back to refinance again to get out of more debt. I also see couples who make good salaries, but don't have enough money to pay their monthly bills on time.

I've come to believe that financial education is the key for everyone. The sooner you start learning about money and personal finance, the sooner you can take control of your own finances. This book will start you off in the right direction and teach you how to build good financial habits. These habits will include spending wisely, saving regularly, and becoming financially independent. When you become financially independent, you control your finances; they do not control you. I'll also share with you all that I've learned during my career in the financial world.

MEET THE TEENAGERS

Throughout this book, I'm going to tell you about five teenagers and how they are managing their money. Perhaps they'll remind you of yourselves at times.

SALLY is 15 years old and has just started working part-time as a cashier at the local grocery store. She works for 12 hours per week – after school and on Saturdays – at $12.00 per hour. Sally always saves part of the money she receives for birthdays and holidays. She currently has over $500.00 in her savings account and will add to this amount from her earnings from her job.

For the past year, 16-year-old GREG has been working on special projects on an as-needed basis at a computer company. Greg likes the income he receives — $500.00 per project. But the company did not withhold taxes from his checks, so now Greg has to come up with the funds to make his April 15 income tax payments to both the federal and state governments. Greg never knew that he was responsible for these taxes, and he never saved any of his money for this purpose. He's learning a hard lesson: What does he do now? How does he pay the governments the money he owes them? How can he plan better for next year, so this won't happen again?

SCOTT is a 17-year-old high school senior. For the first three months of his senior year, Scott worked at an internship offered through his school with a photographer. Now that the internship is over, Scott has decided to continue working with the photographer for as many hours per week he can fit into his schedule. He is thinking about a career in the arts after college and thinks this work will provide a good experience. Scott will be going to college in the fall and is saving as much of his money as he can. His biggest concern is how to afford his first-choice school. The tuition will be over $10,000.00 for the first year alone.

JENNA, at age 14, has started to realize that she needs to have money to get the things she wants. She has just completed a babysitting class and will start to babysit for people in her neighborhood. She is hoping to earn at least $200.00 quickly from babysitting, so she can purchase an iPod Nano. Jenna does get an allowance, but her parents have always taught her to split it into four parts: charity, savings, spending, and taxes. After she buys her iPod, Jenna hopes to split the money she earns from babysitting into the same four parts.

PETER, 16-years-old, can't manage his money. He has worked for over a year as a clerk at a retail store, but he never seems to be able to make his pay last for the two weeks until his next paycheck. He is always borrowing money from his family and friends for one thing or another. To pay back the money, he has to cash each paycheck and distribute the money to his lenders...and then he never has any money left over to do what he has planned to do. This week, he planned to take his girlfriend out for dinner and a movie, but it looks as if he'll be short again. Peter has decided to apply for his first credit card, and he thinks that this will solve his financial problems.

We'll follow Sally, Greg, Scott, Jenna, and Peter as they learn more about finances and managing money and make decisions that affect their financial future. I hope that their stories help you understand the information I'm presenting and help you learn how to make good financial decisions, too.

JILL RUSSO FOSTER

FOR MORE INFORMATION...

This is the first in a series of three books on personal finance. This one deals with issues teenagers face, including how to interact with financial institutions, how to start managing your money, and how to build your credit. The second book builds on this information and adds topics on financial issues facing college-age students. The third book is for young people entering the work world and facing a whole other set of financial issues. I hope you enjoy all three books and learn what you need to know to become financially independent.

From time to time throughout this book, I will refer you to my website (***www.CashCreditandYourFinances.com***) for more detailed information and worksheets. I'll also present updates on financial matters on the website, because the world of finance is always changing. I encourage you to visit my website regularly.

You can also send me questions and comments through my website. In addition, I write a weekly online newsletter called Quick Tips that you can subscribe to for free by going to **www.CashCreditandYourFinances.com** and signing up with your email address.

To get your **Implementation Checklist & Resources Guide**s, please go to **www.CashCreditandYourFinances.com/Guides** to download your free copies.

CHAPTER 1:
BASIC CONCEPTS
PERSONAL FINANCE

MANAGING YOUR MONEY

Whether they know it or not, the five teenagers (see Introduction) are making decisions about managing their money. All are making decisions about how to spend their money. Sally, Scott, and Jenna have decided to save at least part of their money so they can use it in the future. Greg and Peter find themselves in some trouble because they didn't manage their money well.

What do I mean by *managing your money*? Handling it in a way so that you can purchase what you need, pay for important things (like your education), and build a solid financial foundation for yourself throughout your life. Learning about money and personal finances, so you can make good decisions about spending, saving, and investing. Knowing how to work with financial and governmental institutions, so you can use their programs and services wisely and meet all your financial obligations.

You may be thinking, "Manage *what* money? All I have is my allowance!" It's exactly for people like you that I'm writing this book. I'll teach you how to manage your allowance. I'll also teach you how to manage your money so you can make purchases, like an iPod or clothing, or pay for your education. Maybe you'll come to realize that it would be a good idea to get a job, so you'll have some more money. And then I'll teach you how to manage that money, too.

To me, managing money involves setting a budget, establishing savings and checking accounts, building your credit, and becoming responsible for larger, long-term expenses. This is a lot of ground to cover, so let's get going.

TOOLS FOR MANAGING YOUR MONEY

After reading the past 4 paragraphs, I'll bet you think that managing your money sounds very complicated and confusing. Fortunately, there are tools to help you. The most important tool is education. The more you learn about managing your money, the easier it becomes. There are a lot of magazines, books, and websites that can give you information about all aspects of managing your money. On the Internet, you can find discussion groups and bulletin boards, as well as all sorts of advice. On my own website, **www.CashCreditandYourFinances.com**, you can find worksheets and additional information about many of the topics in this book.

There are also commercial software programs that can help you organize and manage your personal finances. The most popular one is Quicken. Another popular one is Microsoft Money. With these programs, you can keep your checking account records, track your savings toward goals, balance your credit card statements, and keep track of all of your transactions.

When you are on the Internet, you may find other programs and websites that say they'll help you manage your money. Maybe they will. But make sure they are legitimate websites before you enter any personal information into them. It's possible that some of these sites were set up by scam artists and identity thieves to get people's personal information. (See Preventing Identity Theft,' below.)

BUDGETING

Budgeting is hard at any age, but the sooner you develop your own budget, the better off you are. You can't have a budget unless you know what your expenses are.

The first step is to track your *expenses,* that is, track every time you spend money. Make a list or create a spreadsheet that shows every time you spend money (including when you use your credit card, get cash from an ATM, and write a check) and organize it by categories. Categories can be as simple as savings, car expenses (gas and repairs), food and meals, education expenses (books, supplies for projects, extracurricular activities), clothing, and gifts. The more specific you are, the easier it will be to see where your money is going. I suggest that you track your expenses for a minimum of two weeks to one month. You will have expenses that are less frequent and have to add them in later (such as your driver's license fee).

Now track your *income*. Start by tracking all sources of income – wages, gifts of money from holidays/birthdays, allowance, and so forth. Figure 1-1 gives an example of a worksheet showing expenses and income for one month. After looking at the example, set up your own worksheet and fill in your expenses and income.

Figure 1-1: An Income and Expense Worksheet
April 2008

Expenses		Income	
Gasoline for car	$160	Allowance	$80
Entertainment	$125	Job 30 hrs@$10/hr	$300
Books and supplies	$55	Babysitting 15hrs@$5/hr	$75
Clothing	$110		
Charity	$5		
Savings	$0		
Total Expenses	$455	Total Income	$455

Which is higher on your worksheet: income or expenses? One of the most important concepts to learn about managing money is that, if you have more income per month than expenses, you are in great shape. You are able to save money on a regular basis. Then you will reach your financial goals. If you spend all your money, as in the example, you won't be able to save for important things.

If your expenses are more than your income, you have to figure out what steps to take that make sense in your life (and it may be a combination of steps). You may have to earn more money to cover your expenses – put in more hours at your job, change to a higher paying job, get a second job, or take other actions. Otherwise you will have to reduce your expenses. You can reduce your expenses simply by spending less in some or all of your categories, or cutting out things that you don't need, or finding lower cost alternatives, and so on. Some examples are using your local library to rent videos/DVDs instead of buying your own. You can bring lunch from home instead of buying it in the cafeteria. I'm sure you can think of more. Another possibility: You can stretch your expenses so they will happen less frequently. If you get a haircut every five weeks, could you stretch it to six? Okay, you think what's the big deal? If you cut your hair every five weeks, you have ten+ haircuts per year. If you lengthen the time to six weeks, you have 8 haircuts per year. This saves you the cost of two haircuts.

Important tip: It's very important to live within your means. The sooner you learn this and do it, the healthier your finances will be.

Included in your monthly expenses should be savings. You need to get into the habit of paying yourself first, by taking some of your money and adding it to your savings. I'll discuss savings more below. You'll also have to include in your budget any debt you are carrying. Everyone carries debt at some point in their lives. Today's society requires that you have and use credit cards to live. You may also find yourself carrying a car loan, student loan, and eventually other kinds of loans, as well. In terms of your budget, the wisest strategy is NOT to carry credit card balances over from month to month. You need to be able to pay off what you charged on your credit cards in full each and every month. Yes, there may be one month when this is not possible. But you don't want to carry large balances and have your hard-earned money go to the credit card company in interest and fees.

Important tip: Get in the habit of saving responsibly and staying within your means. The best use of debt is for the purchase of major items (your home or car), not for everyday expenses.

After you really know what your expenses and income are, you can set a budget. A *budget* is a plan that sets out what income you expect to get and how much you will spend in your various categories. A budget is also a tool that helps you manage your money and reach your financial goals. After you set your budget, the idea is to stick to it. Budgets are no good, if you don't pay attention to the dollar amounts you've entered. Too many people go through the exercise of setting a budget, only to decide a few days later that they *really* want something that's not in their budget and are going to purchase it anyway. And then they don't have money when they need it.

Figure 1-2 takes the categories from Figure 1-1 and establishes a budget that has the goal of saving 10% of income every month. You can see that the budget both increases income and reduces some expenses so the savings goal can be met (or exceeded).

Many people find that they have no idea where their money is going or how much they're spending in certain categories. For these people, the simple exercise of tracking income and expenses and setting a budget is eye-opening. Maybe it will be for you, too.

Figure 1-2: A Sample Budget
May 2008

Expenses		Income	
Gasoline for car	$160	Allowance	$80
Entertainment	$100	Job 35 hrs@$10/hr	$350
Books and supplies	$55	Babysitting 10hrs@$5/hr	$50
Clothing	$100		
Charity	$10		
Savings	$55		
Total Expenses	$480	Total Income	$480

FINANCIAL RECORDKEEPING

It is essential to develop a system of financial recordkeeping that will keep you organized in a way that will empower you for your future. You need to set up a system that works for you now and for the rest of your life.

You'll need to purchase the tools and containers that will hold your records. These can include file folders, boxes, envelopes, and other stationery supplies.

Let's start your recordkeeping system with two file folders. The first one is for your bank receipts, including ATM receipts (which you should get with every transaction), bank deposit receipts, and debit and credit card receipts. The second file folder is for your incoming bills. Open every bill as soon as you receive it to make sure it looks right. Do the transactions on the bill look like the transactions you made over the past month? If yes, put the bill into the bill folder. If not, investigate the transactions that look wrong. Go through your receipts folder to find the receipts for the transactions on the bill. What do your receipts say? Do you even have receipts for the transactions?

If you are still unsure about a transaction and can't get the answers you're looking for, call the bill issuer for more details. This may jog your memory – or you may truly have a transaction that is NOT yours. When you are satisfied that the bill is correct, put it into the bill folder.

As you accumulate more financial documents, you can break down your system further into short-term, medium-term, and long-term records.

Short-term records are receipts, bills-of-sale, invoices, and similar documents that you will be getting rid of shortly. These include receipts for bank deposits, ATM withdrawals, credit card and debit card purchases, and similar transactions. You should keep these receipts until you verify on a statement or bill that the correct amounts have been recorded. For example, a bank deposit receipt should be kept until the deposit is verified on the monthly bank statement and in your checkbook balances. There are two exceptions that will turn a short-term receipt into a medium-term or long-term receipt. The first exception is for a purchase you may want to return to the store. The second exception is for a purchase of a product that has a warranty. After you have verified all amounts and transactions and you determine that you don't have to keep the receipts, shred them (I'll talk more about this in 'Identity Theft,' below).

Another form of short-term record is your paystub. As you receive each paycheck, you should look at it to make sure it is correct. If it isn't, you need to get it corrected (see 'Handling Your Paycheck,' below). When you get your next paystub, you can compare it to the one before to make sure the year-to-date information is correct. I would suggest that you keep one month of paystubs. After that, you can shred the older ones.

Medium-term records are receipts for purchases of major products for which you have product warranties. I suggest you take each of these receipts and staple it inside the appropriate product manual. Then, what do you do with the product manuals? I have a file box for all my product manuals, with file folders for electronics, computers, furniture, outdoor products, and so forth. Simply file your manuals in the appropriate folders. You never know when something will break or stop working and you will have to prove that you are still covered by the warranty. You'll know exactly where to go for your manuals and warranty information. You will keep these receipts for as long as you own the product.

Long-term records include receipts for bigger-ticket items, such as a car. You should start a separate file folder for each of these items. A complete folder for your car should include the purchase paperwork, auto insurance information, and any repair and maintenance receipts.

Some people choose to keep their records, especially the long-term ones, in a safe deposit box in the bank, along with other important documents. You can do this by going to your local bank and renting a safe deposit box. You will pay the bank an annual fee for the use of this box, based on the size of the box you rent, and will be given two keys and a signature card, so you can establish yourself as the authorized signer. To access this box, you will have to sign in and use one of the keys to open it. The advantage of using a safe deposit box is that your important papers will be safe from loss and damage. The disadvantage is that you can get access to the box only during banking hours. If you need certain items regularly, you may want to have another option, such as keeping them in a fireproof home safe.

In addition to your receipts, you may want to put the following items in your safe deposit box: your passport, valuable jewelry that you rarely wear, the title to your automobile, any insurance policies, and any bankbooks.

Records for Preparing Tax Returns. You'll find out how important it is to keep good records when you fill out your tax returns. If you've kept your records in good order in the proper folders, the whole process of preparing your tax returns will be very easy.

The main records you'll need are for income. You'll want to have the yearend paystubs from any jobs. As you prepare your return, you can compare each paystub to your Form W-2, the year-end pay summary you get from each employer, to make sure they agree.

What else do you need to have? You will need to have the Forms 1099 for any interest that you earned on your savings accounts. You will have one Form 1099 for each bank from which you earned over $10.00 in interest in the calendar year.

You typically need to keep all your receipts and other supporting documents used to calculate your income taxes for three calendar years. This means that, when each April 15 comes along and you file your current tax return, you can shred and get rid of the receipts for the tax returns from four years ago. The only exception for this is if you committed fraud. If the IRS accuses you of fraud, they can audit you for seven years.

TAXES

There's nothing sure in life, except death and taxes, the old saying goes. But many people don't understand what taxes they have to pay and what the taxes do for them. In the section on 'Handling Your Paycheck,' below, we'll talk about payroll taxes that are the taxes you pay when amounts are deducted from your paycheck. In this section, I'll discuss some of the other taxes you need to be aware of.

Suppose you are self-employed – you run your own lawn-mowing service. You still have to pay taxes, but they are handled differently. When you work for yourself, you will have to file quarterly *estimated taxes*. These estimated taxes serve the same purpose as the *withholding taxes* on a paycheck; you are paying to the governments (federal and state) a portion of your total income taxes due in the year. If you earn money in the first quarter of the year – January to March – you will have to make a quarterly estimated tax payment in April. Estimated tax payments are also due in June, September, and January of the next year. It is important that you begin to put money away each time you are paid, so you will have the money for these quarterly payments. If you do not make these payments on time, you'll be hit with penalties (you'll owe additional money in late fees and interest). In your budget, make a category for taxes, make sure you save that money, and have that money ready when it is due.

Other taxes may include *property taxes*. Here in Connecticut, we have to pay property taxes on our cars and boats. We are billed once per year and must pay within 30 days. If we don't pay our property taxes when they are due, we will have problems when we try to renew the registration on our cars and boats. You can't drive an unregistered car. If you do and you get caught, your car will be impounded (the police will tow your car and store it at your expense until all your paperwork is complete and all taxes are paid in full). And don't think you can just leave the car in impound and buy another one. You won't be able to register the new car until you've paid everything that you owe on the impounded one.

Another tax in most states is the *sales tax*. When you purchase merchandise or goods, the sales tax is added to your bill, and you pay it automatically. For example, if you go to the store and buy a book, you will be charged the cost of the book, plus a percentage of that cost as sales tax. The same happens for most of the items and services that you buy – if you stay in a hotel on vacation, you will be charged a hotel tax on top of the room rate; if you eat out, a sales tax will be added to the bill.

When it's time to fill out your income tax returns, you can either do it yourself or use a tax preparer. When you first begin to file, your tax returns are relatively simple and you'll probably be filing the short income tax form: Form 1040EZ. You can probably fill this out yourself either by hand or with tax preparation software. If you use the software, you can file the returns online. As your taxes get more complicated and you have more sources of income and expenses, you will be required to file using the long form: Form 1040. You may now want to hire a tax preparer. Once you make that decision, you have two more choices: Go to a tax preparation service, such as H&R Block or Jackson Hewitt; or hire an accountant/CPA. Tax preparation services focus solely on preparing taxes, and it is cost effective to use them; after tax season, they close up a majority of their shops until the next tax season. An Accountant/CPA will cost more, but he or she will be there for you and can assist you at any time during the year.

Greg groaned as he was reading this section. "I wish I had known about taxes before I'd spent all of my money." Unfortunately, Greg has to borrow money from his parents to pay his tax bill, and his parents are planning to deduct the amount borrowed from his allowance over the coming year. This was an expensive lesson for Greg, but now he knows to find out ahead of time what taxes – and other bills – he'll have to pay.

SAVINGS

The most important part of managing your money is saving as much as you can. You probably already have some kinds of savings, but don't even realize it. Most children are given a piggy bank or a jar by a family member to start saving their money. The next step is to develop a plan to make the money you save work for you.

That money sitting in your piggy bank is not earning interest. It is important to learn at an early age that you need to make your money make money, that is, your money must earn interest. Having a bank account is a good way to have your money make money: You save your money in the bank, so your money earns interest and grows.

Think of your savings as accumulating money for short-term things (like going to the movies with your friends), long-term things (like your college education), and emergencies. A good rule is to start to build a savings account for emergencies equivalent to six to eight months of your income. If you do this, you will have the money you need if you face an unexpected expense. Maybe you lose your job and can't find another one right away. Maybe your car breaks down and needs repair. We all face these types of unexpected expenses from time to time, and we need to be prepared by building savings. Think of the benefits of having access to money you saved, as opposed to having to come up with the money in some other way borrowing from a friend or relative, using a credit card to cover an expense, or taking out a loan). It takes planning to get the things that are important to you. If you start saving now, you'll be prepared for whatever happens in your life.

In Chapter 2, I'll tell you about working with banks and opening savings accounts, so you can earn interest. For now, as you read the next sections on handling your allowance and paycheck, remember that it's important to start saving as early as possible and that your savings accounts should earn interest for you.

HANDLING YOUR ALLOWANCE

When your parents give you your allowance, you need to figure out what to do with the money, so you can reach your goals (going out with your friends, buying an iPod, and so forth). You need to think about what you want and need now and in the future. I'm not asking you to think really long-term, but how about next month?

Here's an example: You get an allowance of $20.00 per week every Sunday. You want to take a friend to the movies on Friday, which will cost $25 dollars for tickets and popcorn. The $25.00 is more than your allowance. What do you do? You either have to get more money or make your friend pay for himself or herself – or you don't go to the movies at all.

Important tip: I suggest saving part of your allowance for both short-term things (things you want to have quickly) and long-term things (really big purchases in the future).

. . . .

One way to get on the right track is to start by using envelopes, jars, or other containers. Label them by categories, such as savings, taxes, spending, emergencies, charity, and so forth. Then take your allowance and divide it among these envelopes. This way, you'll know what you have in each category and how much you have to spend. Do you have the money to pay for a purchase in cash? If you don't have enough money, is the purchase really worth it? If so, start to save for it. You will really start to think more about your purchases and determine if they're worth it, if you're paying with your savings.

Is the purchase something that you absolutely can't live without? Or is it a want that you can do without or put off until you have the money?

Important tip: Start to think about your spending, especially in terms of spending your money now versus what you want to do later in life. Learn how to determine if you really *need* something, or just *want* it.

Other options might be to give to charity or invest in long-term savings (investment accounts). Giving to charity (non-profit organizations, such as your place of worship, a humanitarian charity, or a medical/disease charity) with a cash donation or your time is something to consider. Helping others can benefit you, as well as others.

I want to make you aware of *investment accounts*. They can come in many forms, such stock or brokerage accounts or retirement accounts (IRAs, Roth IRAs, 401K or 403B plans). You are never too young to start to invest for your future. The sooner you start to invest on a regular basis, the more money you'll be able to accumulate, because time and interest *compounding* is on your side. Other investment accounts can be used for savings and long term goals, such as buying your first home. I won't talk more about these types of accounts in this book, but you can find more information about them on my website, www.CashCreditandYourFinances.com.

Figure 1-3 shows how our teenagers decided to divide up their allowances.

**How Our Teenagers Divide Up Their Allowances
Figure 1-3:**

	Sally	Greg	Scott	Jenna	Peter
Spending	30%	100%	40%	40%	100%
Savings	50%	0	50%	40%	0
Charity	5%	0	0	10%	0
Taxes	15%	0	10%	10%	0

HANDLING YOUR FIRST PAYCHECK

It's a great feeling to get your first paycheck. Here you are and it's payday, and you are expecting a check for all the hours that you worked. Then you look at your paystub and notice that it is for less money than you thought you'd get.

You think, "What's up?!" In one word, *deductions*. You worked 10 hours at $8.00 per hour, but your check wasn't for $80.00 as you expected. The $80.00 is the *gross amount of your wages* (what you earned before your deductions). Everyone is required to have deductions from their paycheck. You'll see the deductions listed on your paystub. They begin with taxes – federal and state income taxes are deducted (withheld) from each paycheck by your employer. In addition, there is a Social Security (FICA) deduction for when you are eligible for Social Security payments and Medicare, decades in the future. By the way, both you and your employer pay money to Social Security for your future.

When you began working for your employer, you were asked to complete Form W-4 for your payroll deductions. This form asks if you are married or single, how many dependents you have, what your Social Security number is, and other questions. Your answers to these questions determine how much your employer will deduct from your paycheck. The amounts deducted (withheld) from each paycheck are sent to the appropriate government agencies and credited to your accounts (which are identified by your Social Security number) on your behalf. When you file your federal and state income taxes each year, you can apply the sum of your withholding to what you owe. If you have overpaid by having too much withheld, you will get a refund. If you have underpaid, you will owe more in taxes. Your tax preparer will work with you to help you get just the right amount withheld, so you will not owe too much or get so much back. There is a reason you do not want to be eligible to get a huge tax refund: You are in effect loaning that money to the government for the year, and you are not earning interest on it while it is in the government's possession.

Some deductions are optional, such as ones for health insurance, union dues (if you work in a union job), and specific benefits. You can also increase your savings by having an amount automatically deducted from your paycheck and sent to your savings account. This is a great habit to get into. You cannot spend the money that is not in the paycheck. By saving automatically, you will be paying yourself first, and that is how your money will work for you.

Figure 1-4 lists the typical deductions you may see on your own paystubs.

I want to say a little more about Social Security. You may think it's unfair for a deduction to be taken from your paycheck now, when you won't get anything back for many years to come. But think of it this way. Your Social Security deduction is credited specifically to your account under your Social Security number. Every year, you will receive a Social Security statement right before your birthday. This statement will tell you how much you have contributed in the past year. This amount should match any Forms W-2 you get from your employer(s) for the past year. Your statement will also tell you how much you'll get back in payments every year after you retire. Remember that the Social Security program was developed to aid you financially in your retirement years.

Figure 1-4: Typical Paycheck Deductions

Federal income tax
State income tax
FICA (Social Security)
Medicare
Health or dental insurance
401K plan or other retirement plan
Specific optional employee benefits
Savings plan

PREVENTING IDENTITY THEFT

Identity theft happens when someone gets access to your personal information and uses it for illegal purposes. It happens to someone every few seconds. It can be as simple as a friend getting hold of your credit card and making an unauthorized charge or as complicated as someone using your identity to set up a whole new life for himself under your name.

We all have private information that we have to share to get things accomplished in this world. We have to go to the doctor or the emergency room from time to time and have to give our Social Security number and medical information before we are seen. When you apply for credit, you are giving your personal information to a company so they can evaluate your credit worthiness. When you make a purchase from a website, you enter your credit card information; if that merchant's website is not secure or gets hacked into, someone could get your personal information. As you can see, your information is out there in many forms. Sometimes it needs to be, so you can do what you want, like make purchases over the Internet. If that information gets into the wrong hands; however, it can be used for illegal purposes.

So what can you do about it? The first step in preventing identity theft is keeping yourself organized. This means keeping your receipts (paystubs, information with account numbers or personal identification on it, and so forth) from getting into the wrong hands. Start with a filing system to keep your paperwork organized, so you can find it when you need it. Any documents that you're throwing out that have your personal information on them should be shredded. Your personal information includes your name, address, Social Security number, driver's license number, credit card or bank account numbers, and so forth. Never leave this information out in the open or available for others to see. For example, if you're driving around in your car, don't leave your driver's license or wallet in the glove compartment with the car unlocked.

Second, never give out your personal information, unless it's absolutely needed. I recently took my dog to a new veterinarian and was asked on the information sheet to list my driver's license number. I asked why they needed this information, and they said they used the number as identification when people pay with a check. I told them that I would not be using a check and didn't want to list this information. They agreed. How many people have filled out this form without ever questioning the request?

Third, make your passwords and personal identification numbers (PINs) things that you will remember, but are not easy for someone else to guess. No birthdays, no dog's names, no mother's maiden name. Your passwords should include numbers, letters, and symbols and should also be case-sensitive. Don't write your computer passwords on a piece of paper that you have taped to your computer for all to see. Do not write your PIN on your bank card. Never let anyone see you enter your password or PIN.

Fourth, beware of scams, particularly on the Internet. You have probably gotten e-mail messages from people claiming to be banks, PayPal, or official entities that ask you for personal information so they can 'confirm your account' or 'fix a security breach' or do some other legitimate-sounding task. Do not respond to such messages. They are sent by people who want to get your personal information so they can steal your identity.

You may also get telephone calls from people claiming to be from your bank or a credit card company or another official entity. Do not give these callers any information. In fact, do not give personal information out over the telephone, unless you were the one who made the telephone call.

As cautious as you are, you can still be a victim of identity theft. The Federal Trade Commission's website (**www.ftc.gov**) provides information about what to do when your identity has been stolen, particularly who to notify, what steps to take, and how to make sure the problem is fixed.

SUMMARY:

Learning to manage your money well is a skill that will help you build a strong financial future so you'll be able to pay for the things you want.

Budgeting carefully and building a savings plan are your most important tools in managing your money.

If you start to manage your money well now by handling your allowance and paychecks carefully and thoughtfully, you will benefit by being able to make the purchases you need and having the money you need to do what you want to do.

To get your **Implementation Checklist & Resources Guide**s, please go to **www.CashCreditandYourFinances.com/Guides** to download your free copies.

CHAPTER 2:
WORKING WITH A BANK

Bank is a general term that refers to many different types of financial institutions, including commercial banks, savings & loans, credit unions, and now Internet / Virtual banks. In this section I'll tell you about the different types of banks and the products (accounts and financial services,) they offer, and I'll help you chose your bank and work with it successfully.

THE BANKING SYSTEM

The Federal Reserve System
I'm sure you've heard of the *Federal Reserve System*, but do know what role it plays in banking? The Federal Reserve IS the bank system in the United States – it is a bank for the banks and for US Government, and it influences US monetary policy. Think of the Federal Reserve as the umbrella over the banking system. The Federal Reserve is based in Washington, D.C. There are twelve Federal Reserve Banks around the country, each representing a district of the United States. You, as a

consumer, cannot approach the Federal Reserve, but banks can.

The Federal Reserve System was established in 1913 by the US Congress to help make the banking systems safer and more trustworthy. This was a time of uncertainty in the financial markets, and Congress wanted to provide some stability and oversight.

The Federal Reserve System is responsible for managing the money supply and circulating money, among other responsibilities. It gets newly-issued money from the Department of the Treasury and returns old and unusable bills to the Treasury. It sends the money to the banks for use by account holders, circulates and clears checks, and general supervises the banking system.

QUICK FACT: Look at a dollar bill; Do you see a capital letter inside a circle? That letter indicates which of the twelve Federal Reserve Banks issued the bill. Each of the twelve banks has been assigned a letter A – L, and the name of the specific bank can be found in the type in the circle.

Types of Banks
Commercial Banks and Savings & Loans Banks. The first banks in the United States were *commercial banks*, established to serve and meet the needs of businesses. Later, *savings & loans* banks, also known as *thrifts*, were started to meet the needs of individuals in ways commercial banks couldn't. Today, these two types of banks are similar, serving both businesses and individuals and offering similar types of products. Never forget, though, that banks are businesses and are in the business of making money.

Commercial banks are usually larger and have more assets than savings & loans do. They offer the greatest range of products, particularly to businesses, and they are the largest lenders in most financial markets. With changes in banking regulations and a large number of mergers among banks, the largest commercial banks have offices throughout the United States.

Savings & loans are usually smaller than commercial banks and offer a more limited range of services. Their customers tend to be individuals and small businesses. They have the reputation of being friendlier, providing better customer service, and being more involved in local communities than commercial banks. There have been a large number of mergers among savings & loans, too, so many of these differences are disappearing. Both types of banks can meet your financial needs.

Commercial banks and savings & loans have a number of advantages. They have physical offices you can visit to do all of your banking transactions. If you need help, you will be able to talk with people. Both can issue bank cards you can use to make deposits and withdrawals and conduct other routine transactions 24 hours a day at an Automated Teller Machine (ATM). Many of these banks now offer the ability to perform some forms of electronic banking. (See 'Electronic Banking,' below.)

A disadvantage of these types of banks is that you are limited to the individual branch's hours of operation. If you can't get to the branch during these hours, you may not be able to do your transactions or talk with the bank's personnel.

Internet/Virtual Banks. *Internet/virtual banks* are very new additions to the banking marketplace. These banks operate solely over the Internet; there are no physical offices at which you could do your transactions. This has made banking possible from the comfort of your home, via your computer and a secure connection. If you choose to work with an Internet bank, you establish a user ID, open your accounts, and select one or more passwords for access to your accounts.

A main advantage to you, the account holder, is that Internet banks do not have physical locations for you to go to and therefore have lower overhead costs; this advantage is passed along to you in the form of higher interest rates and lower fees. This advantage can also be a disadvantage, though; you may not be able to deal with bank personnel or conduct certain transactions.

Another disadvantage of Internet/virtual banks is that you have to pay attention to security. First, you must make sure that you are using a secure connection; you can tell that your connection is secure if the URL uses 'https,' instead of the usual 'http.' Second, you must make sure that your password can't be guessed easily by others; it should be a combination of letters, numbers, and symbols and should not relate to your life and interests. Your dog's name, 'Skibum,' or 'Salsaqueen' are all out. A third security step is to avoid accessing your Internet/virtual bank account via a public computer; you never know whether malicious software has been installed on the computer, which could steal your account information. Remember, it is much better to be safe than sorry.

A final disadvantage of Internet/virtual banks is that they may not offer the range of services other banks do. Make sure, when you are looking at Internet banks, that they offer the services you will need.

Credit Unions. *Credit unions* are formed for groups of people who have a common interest, such as workers in the same company or teachers in the same school district. Credit union customers are typically referred to as 'members,' because they are part of that specific group and they receive services specifically designed to meet the needs of that group.

Credit unions have many of the same advantages as banks. They too have physical locations, and members can deal with personnel during their branch hours. Some partner with banks, so you can do certain transactions 24 hours a day at ATM machines without incurring a fee. An advantage unique to credit unions is that they typically charge lower fees and provide higher interest rates associated with their accounts.

A disadvantage of credit unions is that they are smaller than many banks, so there are fewer locations to go to. And, of course, you (or possibly a member of your family) may have to belong to the specific group a credit union serves.

Table 2-1 compares the features, advantages, and disadvantages of these types of banks.

The teenagers were very interested to find out about the different types of banks. They had all thought that "A bank's a bank," and they didn't realize that the bank's characteristics and the services offered could vary. Computer-whiz Greg wants to open his savings account with an Internet bank. He's very comfortable with handling transactions over the Internet, and he thinks he knows enough about security issues to keep his account safe. Scott knows that he has to think seriously about his finances, and he wants to be able to ask questions and deal with bank personnel directly. He already has a savings account at a savings & loan, and he thinks it's time to find out more about the services his bank offers. Sally, a good saver already, wants to make sure she is getting a good interest rate at her current bank. Maybe she could get a better rate at a different bank.

Types of Bank Accounts

Banks provide a number of types of accounts, with different purposes, terms, interest rates, and features. If you are considering opening a specific account, you must make sure that you understand exactly what the account is and how you can use it.

Bank accounts fall into two general categories: *checking accounts* and *savings accounts*.

Checking Accounts. *Checking accounts* allow you to keep your money in a convenient and safe place until you need to pay a bill. A checking account is much safer than carrying around a large amount of cash. If you lose the cash, you will probably not be able to recover that money. If you lose your checkbook, you can close your account before someone starts to withdraw money from it.

You write a paper check when you need to withdraw money from your checking account. A paper check is really a way to give your bank written instructions. For example, writing a check to the ABC Company for that $25.00 purchase you made is like telling your bank to transfer $25.00 to the ABC Company.

Many banks offer customers *debit cards* to their checking account customers. You can use a debit card to pay for your purchases, as you would a credit card, but it is essential for you to understand that debit cards work differently from credit cards in two important ways. First, when you use a debit card, the funds are withdrawn immediately from your checking account. So, when you use a debit card, you must make sure that you have enough money in your checking account to cover the purchase. Second, you will be asked to enter a personal identification number (PIN) when you use a debit card, but not when you use a credit card. (Credit cards are discussed in Chapter 3.)

Table 2-1: A Comparison of the Types of Banks

	Descriptions:	Advantages:	Disadvantages:
Commercial Banks	Large, national presence Main customers are businesses	Offer extensive lines of financial services Have many branches throughout country Customers can deal directly with bank personnel	Branches keep bankers hours Often have highest interest fees
Savings & Loan	Smaller, often have only local presence Oriented towards individuals, small businesses and community	Often have lower fees Usually provide great customer service Customers can deal directly with bank	Fewer branches Branches keep bankers hours May not offer full range of services
Internet / Virtual Banks	Virtual banks that conduct business over secure internet	Open 7/24/365 Lower fees	No branches to visit No personnel to deal with

		connections	Higher interest rates for savings	Offer fewer services
			Customers can bank from home	Possibility of security breach over internet connection
Credit Unions	Financial entities serving specific groups of people, such as unions or teachers Customers are *members* of the credit union	Lower fees Higher interest rates on savings Members can deal directly with personnel	Need to be member of supporting group Fewer locations Locations open only certain hours May not offer full range of services

Many banks also allow you to set up electronic banking tied to your checking account. This service allows you to pay your bills through your computer (or cell phone) without ever actually writing a paper check. Again, you must make sure that you have enough money in your checking account when you make an electronic payment.

Savings Accounts. As the name implies, *savings accounts* are used to save money. You put your money in a safe place and earn interest on it at the same time. Generally, savings accounts can be opened with just a small amount of money. Some banks offer under-18-year-olds free savings accounts, that is, accounts that have no fees attached to them.

Remember that savings accounts are used to save money. You should not use the money in your savings account to pay bills or cover monthly expenses. You can make deposits to your savings account at the bank itself or through an ATM.

Money Market Accounts. *Money market accounts* have features of both checking accounts and savings accounts. They are like checking accounts in that you have money on deposit and can draw on that money through the use of a check. They are like savings accounts in that they pay you interest, frequently at a higher rate. These features make money market accounts appealing to many people.

They may not be for everybody, though. To get that higher rate of interest, you usually have to deposit a set minimum balance when you open the account, and you must maintain that minimum balance at all times. You may also be given a maximum limit for the number of checks you can write per month. If you do not have money to create and maintain the minimum balance or if you need to write a lot of checks each month, you may not be able to use a money market account.

Certificate of Deposit. A *certificate of deposit* (CD) is like a savings account in that you can use one to save your money. If you have some money you won't need for a while, you can use it to open a certificate of deposit. When you open a CD, you deposit a set amount of money for a specific period of time. You usually need at least $1,000 to open a CD. Banks usually pay higher rates of interest for CDs. You will not have access to the money in your CD during the period of time you selected. If you do need access to the money in the CD and 'break' it early, you will have to pay a penalty fee. I strongly recommend that you never put all of your savings into a CD; always make sure you have enough available in your regular checking or savings account for your needs.

Bank Services

Banks provide a range of basic services, from savings and checking accounts; to additional financial products, such as certificates of deposit, annuities, and a range of loans; to safe deposit boxes. When you open your account, your bank will give you information about these basic services.

Most banks and some credit unions provide additional services that you may need someday, including bank checks, certified checks, money orders, traveler's checks, and help with investments and financial planning.

Figure 2-1: Services That May Be Offered by a Bank

$ Savings accounts	$ Certified checks
$ Checking accounts	$ Traveler's checks
$ Money market accounts	$ Safe deposit boxes
$ Certificates of deposit	$ Loans
$ Bank cards	$ Electronic banking capabilities
$ Credit and debit cards	$ Help with financial planning
$ Bank checks	$ Help with investments

Bank Checks. A *bank check* is issued by your bank, drawing on funds you give them or have on deposit. The cheapest type of bank check is a *money order*, a check written by the bank for the amount of money that you give them; you fill in the money order and use it to pay a bill or get a service. Each bank has a limit on how much a money order can be worth. If you need a check for more than that amount, you can get a *cashier's check*, which is similar to a money order, but has no limit on the amount. Both of these checks are drawn at the bank where you purchase them, and your receipt is the copy of the check; you will not get a copy of the check after it is cashed. Some businesses ask for a bank check to make sure that your payment is good.

Certified Check. Some vendors will ask you for a *certified check*, to make sure the check will be honored by your bank. If you are purchasing a car, for example, the seller will often request a certified check. You can get a certified check by writing a personal check, taking it to your bank, and asking your bank to certify it. The bank will make sure that the funds are in your account and will then mark your check to indicate that it has been certified.

Traveler's Checks. If you are planning on taking a trip, you can get traveler's checks from your bank. Traveler's checks are 'checks' that are accepted like cash. The benefit of carrying these checks is that if they are lost or stolen, you can get them replaced. Cash would be gone forever. You can get traveler's checks in the currency of the country you are planning to visit. Sometimes a bank will issue a traveler's card, which is like a debit card that you can use to make purchases while you are on a trip.

Safe Deposit Boxes. Many banks offer *safe deposit boxes* to their customers. These are boxes that you can rent and use to store your valuable items, such as the title to your car, your passport, and expensive jewelry that you don't wear often. You have the only keys to your box. In fact, if you lose your key, you will have to pay to have the box drilled open. To access your safe deposit box, you go to the bank during their hours of operation with your key. The bank verifies that you are the renter of the box and grants you access. Remember that you have access to your safe deposit box only during the bank's hours. I have heard of people who are taking a trip forgetting to get their passport out of the safe deposit box until after the bank is closed. You do need to plan ahead.

Bank Fees and Charges

Remember that banks are businesses and are in the business of making money. One of the ways they make money is to charge fees for accounts and services. Your goal is to minimize the amount you pay every month in fees, while getting the highest possible interest. This strategy will help you make the most of your money.

Checking accounts often have a monthly fee and a per-transaction fee. Talk with your bank to find out how you can reduce or eliminate these fees. Sometimes, keeping a minimum balance in your accounts, linking your savings account to your checking account, or arranging for direct deposit of a paycheck (if you have a job) will reduce or eliminate the fees. As a minor, you may be able to have the bank link your account to your parents' account, which could allow you to have an account without fees.

Some of the other fees and charges you may face are for:

1. Depositing a check that is not honored by the bank it is drawn on
2. Writing a check that is not covered by sufficient funds in your account
3. Requesting a 'stop payment order' on a check
4. Using an ATM from a different bank; you could actually be charged fees by both your bank and the bank that owns the machine
5. Overdrawing your account
6. Purchasing a money order, bank check, or certified check

It is your responsibility to be aware of these fees and to avoid as many of them as you can.

CASH, CREDIT, AND YOUR FINANCES: THE TEEN YEARS

Fees on Bounced Checks. I want to say a bit more about bounced checks, because these are a major source of fees and charges.

When you write a check for more than the available balance in your account, the check bounces. Let's say you have $50.00 available in your checking account and you write a check for $75.00. You have overdrawn your account by $25.00, and your check will be returned by the bank for insufficient funds. Additionally, you will incur a fee on your account for writing a check against insufficient funds; that fee will be deducted from your $50.00, so you have even less money than before. Plus, the person to whom you wrote the check will incur a fee for depositing a check that bounces, and that person will want a reimbursement of that fee. This is why it's so important to know your account balance and make sure you have money in your account to cover the checks you write.

Important tip: I know people who bounce checks regularly. They write a check knowing that a paycheck will be deposited into their accounts in a few days. But given electronic banking capabilities, things move faster today. You can write a check in a store today, and within a few hours, the check can hit your account – before your paycheck is deposited – and it will bounce. Get in the habit of having up-to-date, accurate records, so you don't bounce checks.

. . . .

Checks can bounce for other reasons, too. If you mail a check to a person who never receives it, you have to contact your bank to ask for a stop payment order. This order stops that specific check from being cashed when it is presented to the bank. When you place a stop payment order, you are telling that bank that they should not honor that specific check and that you will be replacing it with another check. The bank will charge you for placing the order, and the charge will be deducted from your account.

Choosing a Bank
When you are deciding which type of bank to use, you must decide what is important to you and what services you might need. Some people want to go to a physical bank for their banking business; others are just as willing to work with an Internet bank. You should investigate all of the banks you are considering, compare their advantages and disadvantages, make sure the bank supplies all the services you need, and then make your choice.

Important tip: When choosing a bank, your goal is to minimize the amount you pay every month in fees, while getting the highest possible interest rate.

A general rule when choosing a bank is to find one that has competitive interest rates and minimal fees and is convenient for you in terms of location and hours. The website **www.bankrate.com** is a good source for comparing banks and the interest rates they're offering.

Another general rule is to make sure that the bank you choose is insured through the *Federal Deposit Insurance Company (FDIC)*. The FDIC is a federal agency that insures your deposits in a bank up to a certain amount, so that you do not lose your money if the bank fails. Banks covered by the FDIC will have the FDIC symbol in their ads, on their website, and at the actual branches. Credit Unions are insured by the National Credit Union Share Insurance Fund (NCSIF).

It's a good idea to ask your family and friends where they bank and what they like or dislike about their banks. This information will help you choose which bank is right for you. Or banks; you may have accounts at and use the services of more than one bank.

OPENING AND WORKING WITH BANK ACCOUNTS
How to Open a Bank Account
When you've done your research, selected your bank, and are ready to open your account(s), stop for a moment to double-check these three points:

1. Is this account FDIC insured? If not, don't open the account at that bank, but go to a bank where your account will be insured.
2. Will my checking account be free of fees? You don't want to have monthly charges and fees for your account. Talk with the bank about what you can do to avoid these fees. Sometimes, you can avoid fees by keeping a minimum amount in your account or opening more than one account with the bank or having your paycheck deposited directly.
3. What interest rate will I be paid on my savings account? You want the highest rate available for your savings.

After you finally decide to go with a bank (or banks; remember you can have your accounts at different banks), you have to go to the bank to open the account. The bank will need some identification from you, including your Social Security number and a picture ID (such as a driver's license) to make sure you are who you say you are. You will then have to fill out some paperwork, including a signature card, and turn over your initial deposit. Then your account will be open.

If your new account is a checking account, you often have to wait for your checks to be printed and your bank card mailed to you before you can use the account. This usually takes about two weeks.

As you use your new account, you must also be aware that funds are not always immediately available for use. When you deposit cash into an account, it may or may not be immediately available. If you deposit the cash with a teller, the cash will be immediately available. If you deposit your cash through an ATM, your money may not be available until the next day. If you are depositing checks instead of cash, the rules are different. Your bank will want to make sure that the checks you are depositing clear, that is, that the checks are backed by sufficient funds. If you deposit checks into an account in the same bank the checks are drawn from, the teller will check to see if the funds are available and will deposit the check without a delay. If you deposit a check drawn on a different bank in your state, there will be a delay before the funds are available, while your bank makes sure the check clears. If you deposit a check drawn on an out-of-state bank, the delay is longer. If your deposit a check from a foreign bank, the delay is longer still. You always want to make sure that you have sufficient funds to cover all of the checks you write, so it is important to remember that your bank balance, which includes deposited checks that have not yet cleared, may not be the same as the amount of funds available to you.

Important tip: Check your available balance regularly to find out if the deposits you've made have cleared, before writing checks against them.

....

How to Write a Check. It sounds simple: After you open your checking account, you can just start writing checks. But there are some things you have to know about how to write a check properly.

Figure 2-2 shows a check. You can see that there are a number of spaces that have to be filled in. You write today's date on the 'Date' line. On the line that says 'Pay to the order of', you write the name of the person or entity you are paying. In the box containing the dollar sign, you fill in the dollar amount in numbers. On the next line, you write out the dollar amount in letters. Note that if the written amount and the numerical amount are different, the bank uses the written amount as the amount of the check. At the bottom left of the check, there is a 'Memo' line, which can be used for many purposes. When you are paying a bill, I suggest that you write your account number or the invoice number on the Memo line to make sure your payment is applied to the correct account. (But don't enter your account number if it is also personal information, such as your Social Security number. You never want to write your Social Security number where someone else can see it.) If you are making a purchase, you might want to write what you are purchasing, such as 'iPod,' or any other references that will help you remember what you are paying for. On the bottom right, there is a signature line, which is where you sign your name. You must sign your name the way you signed it when you opened your account; if you opened your account under the name John J. Smith, you must use that name when you sign, rather than J. Smith or Johnny Smith.

Figure 2-2

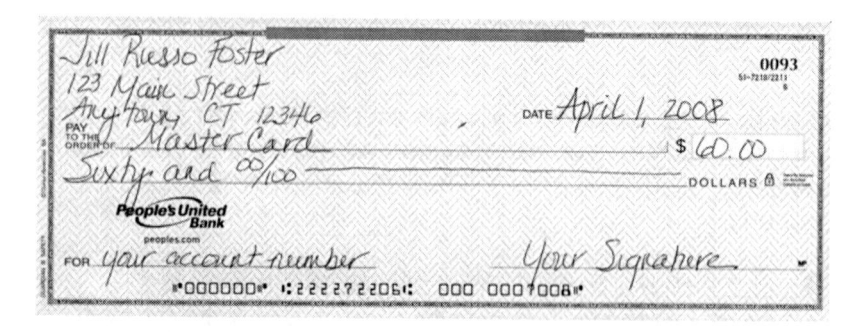

Important tip: Never sign a check that is not completely filled out. If you lose the check, someone else could fill in any amount they choose, and you would lose that money.

. . . .

Keeping Track of Your Checks. It is important for you to keep track of the checks you write. You must take the information from each check you write and enter it into a checkbook *register*. You will receive a paper booklet containing a register along with your checks, or you can use a financial software program, such as Quicken, to keep your register.

Figure 2-3 shows a register page. At the left of the register is a column for the date of the check. The next column is for check numbers. You start your register entry by entering the number

CASH, CREDIT, AND YOUR FINANCES: THE TEEN YEARS

of your check. Make sure that you write your checks in numerical order, so you will know if you have lost a check.

The next columns are for the transactions. Usually, the transaction is the person or entity to which you wrote the check. In your register, you should also list as transactions any fees you paid for your checking account and any ATM withdrawals made from your checking account. It is important to list these items, so you can keep track of exactly how much money you have in your checking account.

Figure 2-3

Transaction Register

DATE	CHECK NO.	CHECK ISSUED TO	IN PAYMENT OF	AMOUNT OF CHECK	√	DATE OF DEPOSIT	AMOUNT OF DEPOSIT	BALANCE
								.00
3/28/08		Deposit	Paycheck				300.00	300.00
4/1	93	Master Card	bill	60.00				240.00
4/5		ATM Withdrawal		20.00				220.00
4/10		Paypal	Ebay purch	35.00				185.00
4/11		Deposit	Cash				45.00	230.00

The next two columns are for payments and deposits. In the 'Payments' column, you list all of the withdrawals from your account; items in this column are subtracted from your account balance. In the 'Deposits' column, you list all of your deposits; items in this column are added to your account balance.

The last column is for your balance. Every time you make a transaction – whether a payment or deposit – it is a good idea to calculate your new account balance and enter that amount into the 'Balance' column. This way, you will know the balance in your account at all times.

Depositing Money. When you receive your checks, you will also receive a number of deposit slips. Figure 2-4 shows a deposit slip. Each time you make a deposit, you need to fill out a deposit slip and submit it with the money you are depositing. Start by writing the date of the deposit on the 'Date' line.

Figure 2-4

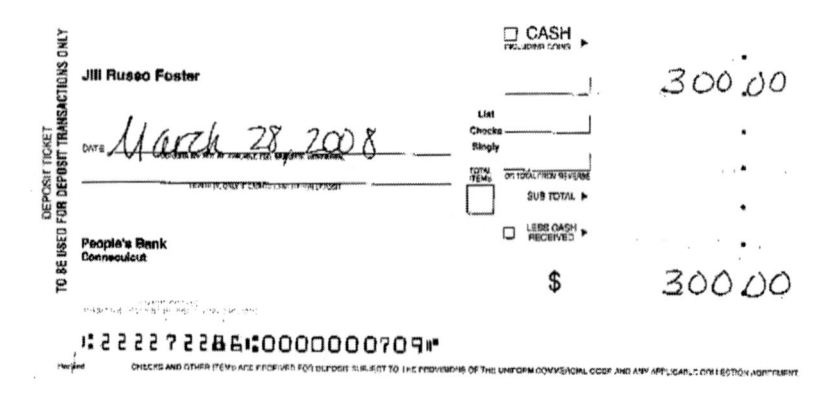

On the line marked 'Cash,' enter the amount of any cash you are depositing. On the lines marked 'Checks,' enter each check separately – one per line. At the bottom of the deposit column, add up all the items you are depositing and enter one amount for the total amount of the deposit. That total amount is the amount you enter in your checkbook register and add to your balance.

When you are depositing checks into your account, you need to endorse each one by signing your name. The endorsement is made on the back of each check. Sometimes there is a line for the endorsement, and sometimes you just make the endorsement where you choose. If you are depositing the checks, write 'For Deposit Only' and sign your name. If you are cashing the checks without entering them into your account, simply sign your name.

Important tip: Never endorse a check until you get to the bank. If you lose a check you have already endorsed, the finder could cash it.

Balancing a Checking Account

Every month, you get an account statement from your bank. When you get the statement, you should perform the task called *balancing your checking account*. This step is important because you can find and correct any errors in your account, and you can keep track of which checks have cleared and what money is available to you.

Your monthly statement covers a set period, often from the first to the last day of the month, but sometimes from, for example, the 15th of one month to the 15th of the next month. Between the time the statement closes (the last day of the set period) and the day you receive the statement, you may make deposits into and withdrawals from your account. This means that most of the time the balance in your register and the balance on the statement are not the same number. To make sure that the account is accurate, you must compare your records to the bank's records over the same time period.

If you keep your register electronically, the program will have a template you can follow to balance your account.

If you are balancing your account manually, you can follow this process: Put a checkmark in your register next to each check and each deposit that shows up on your statement. If you have made transactions that do not yet show up on your statement (that is, you have not put a checkmark next to them in your register), you will have to add or subtract those new transactions from your statement balance to reach your register balance. Start by subtracting all new check amounts from the statement balance. Then add all new deposit amounts to the new statement balance. When you have finished, the new statement balance should match your register balance. If it doesn't, you will have to check your arithmetic and review your statement and the register until you find the cause of the difference.

Important tip: Make sure you balance your checking account every month. It is easier to find errors if you have fewer transactions to check. Plus, some banks may not make corrections after a period of time.

ELECTRONIC BANKING

With electronic banking through your commercial bank or savings & loan, you can bank 24 hours a day, 365 days a year. ATMs were the beginning of electronic banking when they were first installed in the 1980s. Today, electronic banking has expanded to cover a whole range of banking services.

One of the most common forms of electronic banking is *direct deposit* of your paycheck. Even people, who do not use other electronic banking services, sign up for direct deposit.

If you have a job, your employer may ask you to sign up for electronic direct deposit of your wages (paycheck) into your bank account. If you do, you would not get a physical paycheck that you would have to take to the bank to deposit.

Another form of electronic banking is *electronic funds transfers (EFT)*. You may already be aware of this service, but may not know the formal name. When you do an EFT, you are using your money without writing a check. Examples of EFT are shopping online, using a debit card at a store, and transferring money from one bank to another, without going to the bank.

Electronic banking capabilities also let you perform routine banking chores through your computer. You can monitor balances, transfer money between accounts, pay your bills electronically, and get information and some kinds of customer service.

When you are deciding which bank to use, investigate the electronic banking services they provide. When you open your account, sign up for the electronic banking services you want. You can save a lot of time and make your life easier if you take advantage of this technology.

The Check 21 Rule. Even when you write a paper check, you may be using electronic banking without realizing it under a new way of doing business called the *Check 21 Rule*. In the past you would write a check and mail it to the payee, who would deposit the check into his or her account. Funds would then be transferred from your bank to the payee's bank. Under this collection process, the deposit would be in the payee's account, but could not be used until the check cleared.

The Check 21 Rule speeds up the banking process, eliminating the need for the actual check to go from you to the payee's bank and then back to your bank. Instead, the process of clearing a check can be done electronically in just a few hours. You may have seen this process already. If you have paid by check at a store, the clerk may have scanned your check in a special machine. The scanning is the beginning of the Check 21 Rule process, and the payment will be taken out of your checking account as soon as that merchant reconciles that day's transactions.

Important tip: Make sure you have enough money available in your checking account when you write a check. Otherwise, you may incur an 'uncollected funds charge' in your checking account, because there is an *overdraft* in your account. And not just in your account: The payee may be charged a fee by his or her bank, as well, and will probably ask you to pay that fee. Overdrafts can be very expensive.

Greg has already purchased money management software to keep his account records. He's been exploring the software's capabilities and sees he can use the software to set a budget, keep track of how much he's saved toward specific goals, and calculate the growth of his savings account. When he's ready to make investments, he can use the software to keep track of those, too. Greg has spent the past few hours just plugging in numbers to see how savings and investments grow. "This is almost as much fun as a computer game," he thinks.

Sally has had a savings account for a few years, and she thinks it's time to open a checking account as well, because she is starting to have some bills to pay. Sally had gotten in the habit of looking at her paper savings account statement every month and thinks she'll be able to track her checking account the same way. She is ready to use her paper register to keep her records up-to-date and to balance her account.

CASH, CREDIT, AND YOUR FINANCES: THE TEEN YEARS

Summary:
The main types of banks are commercial banks, savings & loans,, Internet/ virtual banks, and credit unions.

Banks offer a range of accounts, including checking and savings accounts. They also offer many services to help you handle your finances, including electronic banking.

When you choose a bank, look for one that provides all the services you need, is FDIC insured, provides no-fee checking, and pays a high interest rate on savings accounts.

To get your **Implementation Checklist & Resources Guide**s, please go to **www.CashCreditandYourFinances.com/Guides** to download your free copies.

CHAPTER 3:
CREDIT AND DEBT

Throughout this country, businesses and people are moving toward a cashless society. People are using bank cards, debit cards, credit cards, electronic banking, and Internet-based services to manage their finances.

Now that you're establishing yourself financially, you may want to move into this world, too. The key is establishing credit and learning how to manage credit and debt. In this chapter, I'll help you understand credit and debt and tell you what you can do to manage both.

ESTABLISHING CREDIT

As you enter the financial world, you'll need to establish your own credit. *Credit* is when you purchase something now and don't pay for it until later. The issuer of the credit extends a certain dollar amount of credit to you (the amount of a loan, or *credit limit*), and you are expected to repay that amount according to the terms of your agreement.

As you go through life and want to make major purchases, such as a car or a house, you'll find that your credit report and credit score, which reflect your use of the credit extended to you, are the keys to your finances. If you use credit well, you may get more favorable loan terms; if you do not use credit well, it may be difficult to get loans at all.

Important tip: Before making a decision to buy or do something, take time to make an informed decision; avoid impulse buying. Think about whether you really need the item, or just want it. Using your purchasing power carefully and selectively may keep you from over-extending yourself into excessive debt.

. . . .

You establish your credit by handling money well. This includes paying bills on time, using your credit cards wisely, and paying back your loans (including student loans) on schedule. Managing your credit cards may be one of the most important things you can do to build credit. Debit cards do not appear on your credit report.

So, how do you establish credit? You must borrow money and then pay it back on time. Many people start out with a credit card; others might take out a small personal loan. If you start with a credit card, you will be given a limit or maximum; you cannot charge over that limit. Then you make a purchase with your credit card, and receive a bill in the mail. You will be expected to pay this bill. The bill will state a minimum amount that must be paid; you may pay the minimum, more than the minimum, or the full amount that you charged. As long as you pay the minimum by the due date, you will be considered in good standing.

The credit card company reports the balance on your account, your payment, and other information to the *credit reporting agencies*. This is the information that appears on your credit report. After a minimum of six months, the credit reporting agencies will rate your credit-worthiness by giving you a credit score (see 'Your Credit Score,' below).

If you choose to establish your credit with a loan, the process is a bit different. You apply to a bank or another lender for a loan, such as a student loan or car loan. The bank may ask you to get a co-signer, because you have not yet established your credit-worthiness. The bank may also ask you to get a co-signer, such as a parent or grandparent, if you are still underage. Then the bank evaluates your loan application to determine whether you are a good credit risk. If the loan is approved, you will be given the loan amount (called the *principal*) to use. This loan will come with a predetermined rate of interest, monthly payment (usually a combination of principal and interest), and length. You will be expected to make your monthly payments over the length of the loan. Your lender will report to the credit reporting agencies whether you make your payments on time. It is essential in establishing your credit to make all of your payments on time. If you are late in even one payment, it will be reflected in your credit-worthiness and your credit score.

CREDIT CARDS

Since credit cards are so important for building credit, you'll want to get one as soon as you can. How do you do this? You start by applying for a secured credit card, which is associated with a savings account. If you have $500 in a savings account that is associated with a secured credit card, you will get a credit card with a $500 limit. You will be able to charge up to your limit.

Every month, you will receive a statement/bill that shows the amount you owe, the items you purchased (called *charges*), any items you returned (credits), the payment you made (a credit), and the minimum amount due by a specified date. All of this information is important to you.

First, you need to make sure that all of the information on the monthly statement is correct. You do this by comparing your receipts to the entries on your statement. If you find a transaction on your statement that you consider incorrect, you must immediately follow the procedure set out by the card issuer for questioning and resolving the problem.

Then, you must make sure that your payment is made before the due date. Depending on the type of card you have, the payment may be the entire amount charged or a portion of that amount. At the very least, you must make the minimum payment specified. The bank must receive your payment before the due date; if you're mailing the payment, you'll need to allow a few days for it to get to the bank. Making your payments on time will establish your credit in a positive way. Remember that, with a secured credit card, the issuer is holding your savings account and can use that money to cover your bill, if you don't make your payments on time.

Credit card billing and payments take into account a *grace period*, which is defined in the terms that apply to the card. The grace period is the time from when you charge to when the bill is due. If you have no balance at the start of the billing cycle and pay the full amount on your current bill by the due date, you are paying your bill within the grace period, and no interest or finance charges will appear on your next bill.

Important Tip: If you do not receive your monthly statement for whatever reason, you are still responsible for paying on time. It's a good idea to be aware of when your credit card payments are due, and be prepared to call the issuer to ask for a copy of the statement. You are not excused from making a payment, simply because you did not receive your statement.

Once your basic credit is established, you can apply for further credit cards at any bank, financial institutions, stores, or companies offering them. Banks issue either MasterCard or Visa credit cards. Individual stores and companies – department stores, gas stations, specialized stores and so forth – all offer credit cards to customers. Financial companies, such as Discover and American Express offer credit cards too.

MasterCard and Visa credit cards are widely accepted. American Express and Discover credit cards are also widely accepted, but some stores accept only certain credit cards. You should check with the merchant before you get to the checkout counter to find out whether your card will be accepted. Cards from individual stores are accepted only at those stores; you cannot use a Home Depot credit card at Sears, for example. When you go shopping, each store may offer you its own credit card; the store may even go as far as offering you an advantage for getting that card, such as 10% off all of you purchases that day.

Important Tip: If is not a good idea to apply for every credit card offered to you; choose wisely, compare terms, and know what you are getting into. Think about how often you would make purchases in that store. Will having the credit card encourage you to purchase more then you need or can afford?

. . . .

Peter decided to go to a local bank and ask for a credit card. He was very surprised when they told him he had to have a savings account with the bank first. "Where am I going to get the money to open a savings account?" he thought. So Peter asked his parents to get him a card by putting him on their credit card account. "I promise I'll pay you back every month," he said. But Peter had already borrowed some money from his mother, and there were no signs she'd get it back. Peter's parents told him they'd get him a credit card after he learned how to stick to a budget. Peter wanted the credit card NOW, though. Some of his friends had gotten credit cards through a nearby big box retailer, so Peter approached them, and was successful. With credit card in hand, Peter bought a new watch for his girlfriend, some new clothes and DVDs for himself, and a cool cell phone as a birthday present for his brother. And then the first bill came. Peter could barely make the minimum payment. He couldn't pay anything on his second bill or the third bill. A month later, the store cut him off and reported him to the credit reporting agencies as a nonpayer. "Now where am I going to get a new credit card?" he wondered.

Credit Card Fees and Terms

How should you determine which credit cards to apply for? You need to evaluate the pluses and minuses of each card. The first thing to look at is the fees associated with the card. Typically, credit card issuers charge several major kinds of fees. The first is an *annual fee* (sometimes called a *membership fee*), which you are charged every year simply for having that credit card. The second is the interest rate you are charged if you do not pay your credit card balance off in full by the due date. You may also be charged fees if you make a late payment (that is, your payment does not reach the issuer by the due date), exceed your credit limit, or pay with a check that is not honored by your bank (due to insufficient funds). Credit card issuers make money from collecting the annual fee, the interest on unpaid balances, and the fees assessed if you violate the terms of the agreement. Many of these fees can be avoided if you pay attention to your finances.

For your first credit card, I suggest that you apply for one without an annual fee and with the lowest possible interest rate. Note that your interest rate can change without notice if you have chosen a variable rate credit card or if you do not comply with the terms of your agreement. Making a late payment or no payment at all can raise your interest rate substantially. You will also fall into *universal default*; this means that anyone extending you credit or services will see that you did not pay on time, so they too will raise your interest rate or change other terms in your agreement with them.

Your monthly bill shows your balance, which includes your purchases for that month, plus any unpaid balance from previous months and the amount of interest you are being charged. The bill also lists a minimum payment; you must pay at least the minimum due. If you pay less than the full amount, you will be charged interest on the remaining balance, even if you pay the minimum amount due.

Credit card issuers tell you how they calculate the interest payment. Some use the *average daily balance method*, in which the average amount you owe on each day is multiplied by the interest rate. Some use a *two-cycle billing average method*, under which they calculate your average amount owed over two billing cycles and multiply that amount by the interest rate. For example, suppose you paid your balance off in full last month, but didn't this month. The balances from both months would be combined and divided by two to come up with the two-month average. I recommend that you stay away from credit cards that use this method of calculating the interest payment.

Some credit cards offer rewards, either on a range of products and services or on specific items. The rewards can be cash back to you, free items, or credit toward certain items, such as airline miles or charitable donations to an entity you choose. Reward cards typically charge both an annual fee and a higher interest rate, since you are getting a reward for using the card. You must read and understand the terms and agreements attached to rewards cards to make sure you get the benefits you deserve.

Using Your Credit Card Wisely
When you have a credit card, you need to be responsible with your finances. This means making charges you can afford, and not charging more than you can afford. It also means avoiding all the extra fees for violating the terms of your agreement. These fees can make the amount you owe even higher and could put you over your credit limit.

Yes, it's very easy to use a credit card – you simply pull it out and hand it to the clerk; you do not have to show identification, as you would if you paid by check. The downside is that you can charge much more than you can afford to pay back. Credit is something you will need throughout your life, and if you get

CASH, CREDIT, AND YOUR FINANCES: THE TEEN YEARS

into trouble by accumulating too much debt and having trouble paying your bills, you can suffer severe consequences. For example, the interest on your unpaid balances will keep accumulating to the point where the interest takes up so much of your income, you can't reduce the balance. Even worse, your account could go into collection (that is, a third party would try to collect the debt), and you would be reported to the three credit reporting agencies as a nonpayer.

There are other problems to be aware of. If your credit card is lost or stolen, it is your responsibility to contact your credit card issuer as soon as possible. You typically have 24 hours to call the issuer to limit your liability to the first $50.00 of unauthorized charges. If you take too long to call, or fail to call at all, you could be responsible for all of the charges. Know at all times what credit cards you are carrying in your wallet, and know where your wallet is. Make sure you keep the paperwork that comes with your new credit card, so you know what telephone number to call to alert the issuer.

Another problem is when an unauthorized charge appears on your bill. The first step is to call the credit card issuer to ask for details of the transaction. Sometimes stores and vendors use a different name (such as the name of their parent company), so you just might not recognize a legitimate charge. If you still don't recognize the charge, you can dispute it. Your credit card issuer will ask you to complete a dispute affidavit and return it to them. The issuer will put the disputed charge 'on hold' until the charge is resolved. The issuer will serve as the intermediary between you and the company that says you made the transaction until the matter is resolved. This is one reason to keep your receipts, keep good records, and compare your receipts to your credit card statements each month – you'll be better able to find errors on your credit card statement.

MANAGING CREDIT

Since it is so important to establish good credit, you will have to pay attention to managing your credit. You can do this by monitoring your credit report, correcting any incorrect information, and doing what you can to raise your credit score.

Your Credit Report

The first step in managing your credit is to check your *credit report* each year. You can order a free credit report from **www.AnnualCreditReport.com**. You are entitled to receive one free copy of your credit report from each of the three credit reporting agencies (Experian, Equifax, and TransUnion) each year.

When you receive the report, take the time to understand the information on it and what the information says about you. Does all of the information apply to you? Is it all accurate? If you find inaccurate information, you need to get it corrected. When you receive the credit report, you will also receive instructions on how to dispute inaccurate information.

Important tip: If you are disputing information on a credit report, remember that the bad information could be showing up on the reports issued by each of the three credit reporting agencies. You might have to dispute the same item three separate times (once with each agency) to clear your record.

. . . .

Correcting or Disputing Inaccurate Information. Suppose the credit report indicates that you made a late payment, but you believe the payment was on time. You may be asked to make copies of your credit card statement and a cancelled check or bank statement that shows the payment was made on time. You would submit this information to the credit reporting agency, so they can investigate the dispute and resolve it in your favor.

What if you find an account listed on your credit report that is not yours? It's impossible to prove that an account is NOT yours, so you would have to ask the credit reporting agency to investigate and to compare your personal information with the paperwork the account issuer has on file. It is possible the account issuer confused you with someone else. This is very common when a family gives a son the same name as the father (such as John Smith, John Smith, Jr., and John Smith III).

Because I'm in the mortgage business, I see many credit reports, and I would estimate that half of them contain at least one error. Correcting the error can make the difference between getting what you want financially and being denied credit or offered less-than-favorable terms. So make sure that you correct any errors on your credit report by following the instructions.

An investigation by a credit reporting agency into a dispute can have one of three outcomes:

1. You have proof that an error has been made, and the dispute is resolved in your favor.
2. You don't have proof and are relying on the entity making the charge or issuing the credit to have the information; this dispute may not be resolved in your favor.

3. The credit reporting agency does not get a response from the entity making the charge or issuing the credit, and it is up to the agency to make the decision.

The credit reporting agency typically takes 30 days to resolve any dispute. When you are working with an agency, make sure you keep copies of all of the paperwork you send them, along with their responses.

If you think you are a victim of identity theft, see 'Preventing Identity Theft' in Chapter 1 for information on handling this problem.

Your Credit Score

One of the most important lessons to learn from this book is how important it is to know and understand your credit score. A *credit score* is a three-digit number used throughout the financial industry to determine a person's creditworthiness. A company called Fair Isaac and Company (FICO) developed the standard formula used by the three credit reporting agencies to assign a credit score to each person's credit report.

Credit scores range from a low of 350 to a high of 850. The average creditscore is 720. Lenders often look for a score of 760 or higher.

Your credit score is an extremely important number. Your credit score determines whether you will get the credit you are applying for and what the interest rate will be. Your credit score may be used by landlords to determine whether to rent an apartment to you. Potential employers may check your credit score to help decide whether to hire you for that job opening. Car dealerships will certainly check your credit score before deciding whether to give you a car loan and what interest rate to charge.

CASH, CREDIT, AND YOUR FINANCES: THE TEEN YEARS

So, how do you get and maintain a high credit score?

Under the FICO formula, your credit score is determined by the following five factors:

1. 35% of your score comes from your payment history. How do you pay your bills: On time? Late? Not at all?

2. 30% of your score takes into account the total amount you owe in relation to your credit limits, that is, how much you've already borrowed in relation to how much money you could borrow. The amount you've already borrowed should be less than 50% of what you could borrow.

   For example, suppose you have two credit cards, each with a credit limit of $1,000.00. The total amount you could borrow would be $2,000.00. If you already owe $500.00 on one card and $250.00 on another card, the total amount you've already borrowed is $750.00. Therefore, you already owe $750.00 against a credit limit of $2,000.00, or 37.5% of your credit limit.

3. 15% of your score comes from the length of your credit history. The longer you have a credit card, for example, the more history you accumulate, and the better sense a borrower gets of how you handle money. If you've just gotten your first credit card, a borrower might not be able to tell how good a payer you would be.
4. 10% of your score is based on how many new accounts you've opened and recent credit applications you've made. Any time you authorize someone to review your credit report for the purpose of extending credit, your credit score is reduced by a few points. So, if you apply for a number of new credit cards and open a number of

new accounts over a short period, your credit score could be lowered.
5. 10% of your score is based on your credit mix, that is, how much of your credit is secured and how much is unsecured. *Secured credit* is based on something of value to support the loan. A car loan, for example, is secured by the title of your car. A credit card can be either *secured* or *unsecured credit*.

Now that you know how a credit score is calculated, you can easily see how to establish and maintain a high score: Pay your bills on time. Don't spend up to your credit limits all the time. Manage your use of credit over time. Don't open too many credit card accounts. In other words, managing your finances well generally will help you manage your credit well.

Important tip: Keeping your credit score as high as possible will benefit you in all aspects of your financial life. Your score affects everything from getting a credit card, to renting an apartment, to the amount you will pay to insure your car, to being offered a job you really want...and more.

. . . .

MANAGING DEBT

If you can manage and pay for your debt, all is well. If you can't, bad things happen quickly. It's hard to get out of debt if you have charged the maximum amounts on all of your credit cards and are close to your credit limits. This is a negative factor on your credit report and will lower your credit score. (See the section on 'Credit Scores', above.) This in turn, makes it much more difficult to get another credit card.

Suppose you have accumulated a lot of debt and need to reduce it. What do you do? The first step is to make a list of all of your credit cards and any other types of debt, including the name of the credit issuer, the minimum payment amount, the total balance owed, the interest rate, and the credit limit. The second step is to make sure that you make at least the minimum payment to each credit issuer every month before the due date. The third step is to pay more than the minimum amount to credit issuers when your balance is over your credit limit and you are being charged additional fees. When you bring your balance under the limit, the fees will be reduced.

When all of your credit account balances are under their limits, start making extra payments to the credit issuer charging the highest amount of interest. Use any extra money you have and add it to the minimum payment until this balance is paid off in full. Then start paying extra money to the credit issuer charging the second highest rate of interest. Continue to do this until all of your credit accounts are paid in full.

Paying down debt will require that you budget carefully (see the section on 'Budgeting' in Chapter 1 for more information) and that you watch your day-to-day spending. You may have to put in more hours at your job, get a second job, or get a higher-paying job. You will have to watch every penny that you spend to see where you can come up with the extra funds. This can be very difficult for you, but the rewards down the road make it more than worthwhile.

When you are carrying too much debt, you will find it very hard or impossible to get new credit. If you do get new credit, the interest rate will be extremely high. Credit card interest rates tend to fluctuate and can be as low as around 8% for people with excellent credit to as high as 30% for people with not-so-good credit.

If you are carrying a credit card balance of $5,000 at an 18% interest rate, it will take you over 18 years to pay off the loan if you only pay the minimum amount due with each statement. Clearly, making sure you keep your interest rates as low as possible and making more than the minimum payment will help you keep your debt manageable.

Important tip: If you accumulate too much debt, you may not be able to make the purchases you want. If you spend up to your limit on your credit cards, the money won't be available to purchase the new iPod, for example. Also, utilities and some services may check your credit score before allowing you to sign up. This is especially true for some telephone and communications services. So make sure that you keep your debt to a level you can easily handle.

BORROWING FROM OR LENDING TO A FRIEND

Borrowing from or lending to a friend can be tricky. Let's say you have a friend who wants to borrow $20.00 from you. You do lend him the money, with the understanding that he will pay you back in two weeks when he gets paid. In two weeks, the friend does pay you back. All is well. But what happens if the friend can't pay you back, or simply doesn't pay you back in two weeks? Not only will you be out your $20.00, but you could also lose a friend. I suggest you think hard about lending money to friends.

Let's look at the other side: Suppose you want to borrow money from a friend. You need to be absolutely sure that you can pay this person back when you say you will. If you ever watch the court shows on television, you'll see a lot of cases about someone borrowing money from a friend or family member and not paying it back. The two parties end up in court, and usually the relationship is broken. Is losing your relationship with a friend worth borrowing the money?

If you do choose to borrow or lend, I suggest that you put it in writing. You should write out an agreement, so that everyone is clear about all the terms. Here's a possible agreement:

I, John Smith, am borrowing $100.00 from George Jones for football tickets and will repay the loan by paying $20.00 per week starting on January 5, 2009, and making a total of five payments over the next five weeks.

This agreement states the amount of the loan, the terms of repayment, and the timing of repayment. Both you and the person borrowing or lending the money should sign the agreement and you should each have a copy.

If you lend money to a friend and he defaults on repayment, you will have to make a decision. Perhaps you have extra money and are willing to convert the loan into a gift. Or perhaps you could extend the loan by allowing your friend to repay it later. But you should be prepared for the possibility that your friend will not repay the loan, and you will have to decide whether you will take any further action.

Summary:
Establishing credit means handling money well, including paying bills on time, using credit cards wisely, and paying back loans.

Credit cards are available through banks, financial companies, and stores. Before taking out a credit card, make sure you understand the fees and terms attached to it.

To manage your credit effectively, check your credit report every year, correct any inaccurate information on it, and monitor your credit score. If you do accumulate debt, set a schedule for paying it off.

To get your **Implementation Checklist & Resources Guides**, please go to **www.CashCreditandYourFinances.com/Guides** to download your free copies.

CHAPTER 4:
PAYING FOR YOUR EDUCATION

Paying for your education after high school can be expensive, but you have a number of options. This is a broad area, with many sources of funds and many strategies to consider. In this chapter, I'll tell you about the basics and suggest where you can get more specific information about the options that may be best for you.

There are many sources of information about funding for your education. The US Department of Education website provides information about federal government programs. Your state government website will discuss programs available specifically in your state. The Financial Aid Offices of the colleges and universities you are applying to can tell you what aid is available from the school. Your high school guidance counselor can tell you about aid from local businesses, service clubs, and other entities. The Student Loan Marketing Association (Sallie Mae) website discusses the whole application process and provides information about specific programs. As you develop your plans, you should take advantage of all of the free information available to you, and you should investigate all of the possibilities. You can find more information about sources of information on my website: **www.CashCreditandYourFinances.com.**

As you read through this chapter, remember that the funding you arrange will have to cover a lot of expenses, including:

- ✓ Tuition
- ✓ Room and Board
- ✓ Fees from your school
- ✓ Books and supplies
- ✓ Transportation costs
- ✓ Your personal expenses

You may be able to get funding to cover some of these costs, but not all. Some sources may cover only tuition, and some may cover all of the bills from the school. Even when you get as much money as you can from all of the sources, you may still have to work to cover your personal expenses.

Scott's eyes widened as he read about all the expenses he'd have to cover. He realizes that he is going to have to get a substantial amount of support to get the education he wants. He does have good grades and, because of his internship, he has been able to put together a portfolio of his work. Now, he needs to figure out how to pay for his schooling.

STRATEGIES FOR PAYING FOR YOUR EDUCATION

There are many ways to pay for your education, including savings, scholarships, loans, financial aid, and work/study programs. Most students combine several of these options when creating their financial package.

Savings

Your first step is to find out from your parents whether they or other relatives have done anything to pay for your education. They may have started a college fund for you or they may have taken advantage of some of the savings programs that are available. These programs include:

- 529 plans, through which your parents can save a certain amount of money each year, without having to pay taxes on it.

- Pre-paid tuition plans, which are sponsored by some states and colleges, through which your parents can start paying your tuition years before you actually go to college at the rates charged at that time. These plans may require you to be a resident of a specific state or to go to a college in that state.

- Trusts specifically set up under the Uniform Transfers to Minors Act or Uniform Gifts to Minors Act to fund your education.

It may not be too late even now for your parents to take advantage of these programs.

If some of the funding will be paid by your parents, they can take advantage of two programs: the HOPE Scholarship Tax Credit, and the Lifetime Learning Tax Credit. Both of these credits allow them to save on their income taxes by deducting certain amounts of the money they pay toward your education.

Scholarships

Scholarships are given by schools and organizations and are worth a specific amount of money towards your education. Many scholarships are *need-based*, that is, your family has to demonstrate that it needs the money. Other scholarships are *merit-based*, given for academic achievement, special talents, or athletic ability. A *full scholarship* to a college pays your tuition and sometimes other bills in full. Because full scholarships are worth so much money, there is a lot of competition for them. You could also receive a *partial scholarship* worth a specific amount; you would then need to use other means to finance the rest of your education. The best thing about scholarships is that you do not have to repay the funds, as you would for a loan.

Some companies and organizations offer scholarships based on varying criteria. The company your parent works for may offer a scholarship for the education of an employee's child. Civic organizations offer them, as well. Many scholarships have criteria that you need to meet in order to apply, such as specific interests or achievements. Scholarships through the Reserve Officers' Training Corps (ROTC) may be available at certain schools for students willing to make a commitment to the military.

Most scholarship programs will require you to complete an application and could require you to write an essay. Each one will have different requirements that you will need to follow.

Loans

Another option is applying for *loans*. As the name states, these are loans, and you will need to pay them back. Most families can qualify for loans under programs offered by the federal government, state governments, and private lenders.

Some loan programs allow students to take out loans in their own names – called *student loans* – but depending on your credit rating, the lender may ask you to get one or more of your parents to co-sign. Student loans are usually for small amounts of money, with maximum limits set by the loan program. They are usually just for one semester or one year, and you will have to reapply each and every year you are in college to renew or extend your loan. You could end up with several student loans by the time you graduate. A benefit of student loans is that they will not have to be paid back until you graduate or leave school.

Sometimes the loan is in your parents' names, not yours. These are called *parent loans*, and they are very common. Another option is to take out a private loan from a financial lending institution. The majority of students who attend college will end up with some type of loan to repay when they graduate.

The most popular and least expensive student loans are from the federal government. These loans have the lowest interest rates and are not granted solely to people with good credit ratings. There are basically two types of federal government student loans: subsidized and unsubsidized. Under *subsidized loans*, the government pays your lender the interest on loans from other sources while you are in school. Subsidized loans are typically given to people who have a financial need, such as students from low-income families. If you qualify for a subsidized loan, you might find this to be your best option.

If you do not qualify for a subsidized loan, you can get an *unsubsidized loan*, under which you pay the interest to the lender. Therefore, if you get an unsubsidized loan, you will wind up owing the lender more money (because you will be paying interest) and will have more payments. Remember that you can usually have the lender defer the payments until you are out of school.

You can take out both subsidized and unsubsidized loans. For example, you can get a partial loan that is subsidized and then get the additional funds you need through an unsubsidized loan.

Financial Aid

Financial aid is another option. You get financial aid from the school you are going to attend. The aid is based on a number of factors, including family income and assets, family expenses, the number of children in college at the same time, and the student's savings and earnings. Schools may also take into account any special circumstances, such as outstanding athletic ability, talents, accomplishments, and academic record.

Work/Study Programs

Individual colleges may provide work/study programs. Under these, you work for a certain number of hours at a campus job, and in exchange you will be given either credit towards the cost of your education or a salary.

Table 4-1 compares these options. Many students combine these programs to get as much assistance as possible to cover educational expenses. (See Figure 4-1)

Figure 4-1: Examples of Combining Funding Options

Student 1:	Student 2:	Student 3:
No funding from parents; qualifies for need-based programs	50% parents' savings under 529 plan	25% grandfather saved for student's education
50% scholarship from school	35% parent loan	50% academic scholarship
45% government subsidized loans	10% work/study program	20% unsubsidized student loans
5% on-campus job	5% student savings	5% on-campus job

TYPES OF STUDENT LOANS AND FINANCIAL AID PACKAGES

Federal Government Programs

The federal government supports a number of different loan programs, with different characteristics, criteria, and terms. Almost everyone qualifies for one or more of these programs, and you should investigate them all to figure out which is best for you. The loans in these programs can come from banks and other lending intuitions; they can be insured by the federal government or guaranteed by state agencies. The loans can either be in the student's name or the parents' names.

Student loans from the government have a maximum loan amount for each school year; currently the maximum amount for a freshman is $3,500 and for a sophomore is $4,500. If your loans come from the government, you will have to combine the loans with other financing options to get the amount you need.

Table 4-2 lists and defines the major federal government loan programs.

Another option is to take advantage of Veteran's Benefits Programs offered to students who have served in the branches of the military.

You should know about the Student Loan Marketing Association (Sallie Mae). Sallie Mae was founded in 1972 as a government-sponsored entity, but is now a private company. On its web site, **www.SallieMae.com**, you will find lots of information about types of loans, grants, and scholarships; the application process; and strategies for managing and paying back your loans. Sallie Mae can also help you repay your loans by consolidating them into a single debt and by arranging an extended payback period.

State Government Programs

The fifty states all provide some sort of support for students, but the benefits may be restricted to state residents or to students attending school in the state. Some of the programs are aimed at encouraging students to get degrees in particular programs to service the needs of the state, such as nursing, business and finance, or high technology.

Table 4-1: Options for Funding Your Education

Strategy	Description	Advantages	Disadvantages
Savings	529 Plans	Easy way to accumulate funds over many years	May be residency or school requirements
	Pre-paid Tuition plans		
	Trusts	Can cover	

Scholarships	Full or partial scholarships cover portions of your education costs	substantial portion of costs No need to repay	May be eligibility criteria May need to maintain good academic record
Loans	Money extended by federal and state government and private lenders	May defer repayment	Need to be repaid Need to reapply every year Need to maintain good academic record
Financial Aid	Granted by a school	No need to repay	Need to meet eligibility criteria
Work/Study Program	Work at a campus job to get credit towards cost of education	Job can provide academic or practical experience	

Table 4-2: Major Federal Government Loan Programs

Program	Description	Need based	Repayment	Other Features
Stafford Loans	Federal direct student loans or guarantees of loans from other lenders	If subsidized, yes If unsubsidized, no	Starts 6 months after student graduates or leaves school	Set maximum amount per year
Parent Loan for Undergraduate Student (PLUS)	Federally funded or guaranteed parent loans made by other lenders	No	Starts immediately	Can borrow up to total cost of education
Pell Grants	Federally authorized grants up to defined amount for neediest students	Yes	No need to repay	Set maximum amount per year Programs not fully funded
Perkins Loans	Federal low interest loans for neediest students	Yes	Starts 9 months after student graduates or leaves school	Set maximum amount per year Repayment may be deferred or extended

The programs vary by state, with some states providing a lot of aid and some less aid. You can find out about these programs through your state's higher education office.

School Programs

Financial aid packages from schools often combine scholarships, loans, and work/study programs. Sometimes schools have arrangements with specific lenders to get favorable rates and terms.

Certain schools may be interested in making it easier for their students to pay for their educations. They may work with your parents to do such things as spreading out payments over the entire year, instead of demanding payment at the beginning of each semester. Or they may allow parents to prepay four years of costs at the current rate.

Your school's financial aid office will be able to give you a package of information that will explain what support is available and how to apply for the aid. It's also a good idea to ask your school about any criteria for getting or keeping aid. For example, some schools may offer aid only to full-time students or only to students with certain grade point averages. Some schools may also require students to start repaying loans if they take time off.

Private Programs

If you do not qualify for government loans or need additional money, private loans are your next option. Most financial lending institutions, including banks and credit unions, offer education loans. These loans, which may be student loans or parent loans, usually have a higher interest rate, which is based in whole or in part on your credit score. This is another reason to make sure that you are managing your credit.

Sometimes, lending institutions work with parents on home-equity loans or home-equity lines of credit that can be used to finance your education.

In addition to loans, some private entities offer grants or scholarships, for which you may qualify. These entities include the companies your parents (or you) work for, labor unions, and charitable trusts and philanthropies.

The criteria for these scholarships vary. A parent may have to work for a specific company or belong to the union. Or you may have to be pursuing certain degrees or have done volunteer work or have specific interests. It's a good idea to start researching these private programs as early as possible, so you can figure out whether you qualify for any.

Scott decided to talk with his parents. He learned several things: His grandfather had been saving some money towards Scott's college education, but as college expenses have been rising quickly, this fund would pay for only about 25% of his education at his first-choice school. Scott's parents also explained that Scott could not qualify for any need-based programs. Scott's father suggested that they go to the savings & loan, where Scott and his parents have their accounts, to talk with one of the loan officers. The loan officer was very helpful and told Scott and his parents a lot about loan programs and how the programs would actually work. When Scott and his parents got home, they decided to read about some of the specific programs the loan officer suggested on the Internet. Some of the funding pieces were starting to fall into place.

STANDARD TERMS OF LOAN PACKAGES

Any loan you or your parents take out for your education will come with a set interest rate. Your interest rate on a private student loan may be reduced if you have a co-signer, such as a parent. This is something you should discuss with a parent, along with the advantages and disadvantages of having a co-signer, to see if this option makes sense for you.

The loan will also define the payment terms. Under the terms of many government and private student loans, payment may be deferred, so you won't have to make payments while you are in school. You can apply for the deferment while you are in school to postpone your payments until you graduate or leave school. You can also apply to defer the payments if you are continuing on for more education in graduate school. Parent loans typically cannot be deferred; your parents will have to start making payments on their loans shortly after they receive the money.

If you leave school or take a leave of absence, you will be in the *grace period* before you have to start repaying your loan. This grace period is different with each type of loan. When the grace period passes, you must begin to make your payments. It is important to know what your loan grace periods are and to keep them in mind when you are considering your future. For example, you may not be able to take off for a year of backpacking around the world if your grace periods expire in six months.

When you read Chapter 5, you'll learn that minors cannot sign legal contracts. There is an exception for student loans, though. In 1992, the federal government passed a law stating that, if a student meets certain requirements, that student could sign a note for a higher education loan. This exception applies only to certain government loans, and not to private student loans.

Important tip: It is essential that you understand all of the terms of your loan programs. Do not assume that the terms for one program apply to all your loans. Make sure you understand what your responsibilities would be under each program. Before you sign your loan contracts, you need to know what you will be expected to do, and you need to think that you can meet all of the requirements.

HOW TO APPLY FOR SCHOLARSHIPS, STUDENT LOANS AND FINANCIAL AID PACKAGES

Qualifying for Scholarships, Loans, and Financial Aid

Generally, you can increase your chances of getting help paying for your education if you:

1. Maintain good grades and score well on the standardized tests, such as the SAT and ACT. Many types of student loan, scholarship, and financial aid packages are based on your academic record.
2. Maintain a good academic record while you are in college. Remember that you will have to reapply for loans every semester or every year, and the lenders may want to see a certain grade point average or course load (for example, a 3.0 grade point average and 30 credits). If you do not meet the minimum requirements, you may not be able to get additional financial aid or another student loan.

3. Maintain a good credit rating. If you have taken out a credit card and have paid all your bills on time, you will have established good credit, which could get you favorable rates on student loans. Some colleges may also check your credit rating before putting together a financial aid package for you.

Applying for Scholarships and Financial Aid

If you are trying to get a scholarship or financial aid from your college, you will have to request it when you submit your application. Your college will have a standard form and procedures, which you must follow. Your college will also ask for specific supporting material. Make sure you pay attention to all deadlines and get all forms and information in on time. It's a good idea to submit your application as early as possible. Sometimes colleges have a set amount of money to distribute or a set number of work/study jobs to allot; when they've distributed everything, there is no more for late applicants. You improve your chances of getting a favorable financial aid package if you're at the head of the line.

Applying for Federal Government Student Loan Packages

You and your family will have to complete the Free Application for Federal Student Aid (FAFSA) form for each school year that you will need financial assistance. This form is then submitted to the US Department of Education for use with all federal programs. The information on the form will help determine how much loan and grant money you qualify for and how much the government thinks your parents should contribute.

You usually have to complete further applications for specific student loan and financial aid packages. This typically cannot be done before January 1 of any given year, because you will be required to provide your tax information for the previous year. Many schools and loan programs have deadlines, which can be as early as mid-February or March 1, so you will need to act quickly to apply.

Applying for Loans from Financial Lenders

If you apply for either a student loan or a parent loan from a financial lender, you will have to follow that lender's standard practice. You or your parents will have to fill out applications and provide all the supporting documentation requested. Remember that you will have to apply for new loans every year, so it is important to maintain good relations with your lender.

Applying for Scholarships or Grants from Other Entities

The other entities that give scholarships and grants will each have their own application process. You will usually have to fill out an application that demonstrates why you qualify for the aid. Frequently, you will also have to write an essay related to the interests of the entity. As with all other aid programs, you must make sure you fill out all the required forms and submit all the information they request. And you must make sure to meet all the deadlines.

In September of his senior year, Scott decided which colleges to apply to, and he requested information about any school-based financial aid and work/study programs. As soon as they could, Scott and his parents filled out and submitted the FAFSA. They also filled out financial aid forms from the colleges, and Scott indicated on his application that he'd like to get an on-campus job. As April approached and Scott would receive his acceptance letters (he hoped they'd be acceptance letters), Scott felt confident that he would get the financing he needed. He had done his research, understood what he could apply for, and filled out and submitted all forms on time. He really started to look forward to pursuing his goal of a career in the arts.

PAYING BACK YOUR LOANS

Eventually, you will graduate or leave school, and it's time to start paying back your loans. At this point, you must make sure you understand the terms of your loan, so you know what is expected of you.

Some students used to feel that they could just default on their student loans. I strongly recommend that you remove that thought from your head. Your credit would be ruined at just the time in your life that you'll want to get more. If you default on your loans, you might not be able to buy a car or a house or get insurance or even hook up the utilities in a rented apartment. Moreover, the lenders have a lot of tools to get their money back from you. They can have your paycheck garnished, get court judgments against you or even have you charged with a crime. You don't want any of this to happen.

Important Tip: You can improve your chances of being able to put together a good education funding program by getting good grades, building a good credit rating, and establishing a good record.

Fortunately, most lenders are willing to work with you to make it easier to repay your loans. You may be able to arrange for a longer grace period or a longer payback period or smaller monthly payments.

Remember that paying back your loans, including all your student loans, is an essential part of building and maintaining your credit, If you handle your student loans well, you will find it much easier to get the credit that you need as you proceed through life.

> **Summary:**
> Students can pay for their college education and graduate school through a combination of scholarships, financial aid, student loans, parent loans, and work / study programs.
>
> When you apply for these types of assistance, you will have to provide financial information and show that you meet the terms of the particular program, whether need, academic achievement, interest, or other qualifying factor.
>
> To increase your chances of getting the assistance you need, it is important to maintain a good academic record and a good credit rating.

To get your **Implementation Checklist &Resources Guide**s, please go to **www.CashCreditandYourFinances.com/Guides** to download your free copies.

CHAPTER 5: MAJOR PURCHASES

Part of the fun of saving money and establishing credit is being able to purchase items that you want. It is smart, though, to learn about making purchases so you don't spend more than you have to, but do establish favorable payment terms and manage your debt wisely. First, you have to learn about contracts.

ABOUT CONTRACTS

A *contract* is an agreement between two parties. A contract can be as simple as

> "I will buy your 2005 Honda Accord for $5,000.00, with a down payment of $2,000.00 and monthly payment of $200.00 until the balance is paid in full."

In this simple contract, you and someone else are agreeing to all of the terms.

Contracts can be verbal between the two parties, but sometimes the parties do not remember the terms in the same way, and sometimes verbal contracts cannot be enforced. I strongly recommend that you write your contracts down on paper, with both parties signing, dating, and receiving a copy.

Some contracts are very simple and the two parties can write the terms themselves. Others are more complicated, and it's wise to hire an attorney to write the contract. The contracts car dealerships use are written by attorneys and contain many legal clauses to comply with federal and state law.

You would never purchase a car from a dealership with only a handwritten agreement.

Contracts need to include some basic information to be valid. The basic information includes:

- Names of the parties involved
- Date of the contract
- Details of the terms
- Signatures of all people involved

Depending on the type of contract and location of the agreement, there can be other requirements. For example in the State of Connecticut, a building contractor must put specific wording into a contract, or the contract will not be enforceable. Each individual state has specific requirements for various types of contracts, and you would be wise to look into the requirements before you try to write a contract on your own.

I'm familiar with the need to look into requirements myself. I am a landlord and rent an apartment to another person. When creating the rental agreement, I start with the basic forms that you can buy at any office supply store and then have an attorney add in any specific clauses needed in my state. I do this so, if I need to go to court to enforce that contract, I know I will have a legally-binding document.

You may have watched one of the televised court shows. Most of the cases in these shows involve an agreement, with one person saying the agreement states this and the other person saying the agreement states that. Usually, the people who win are the ones with the proof. The written contract is the start of establishing the proof, so get in the habit of having written proof – a valid contract – and keep that proof in a place where you can find it when you need it.

Now you know what a contract is...but can you enter into one? The short, simple answer is "No." You must be of legal age to enter into a contract by yourself. You could enter into a contract if your parents sign on your behalf. If they do, though, they become the party legally responsible for carrying out the terms of the contract. That is, they may wind up having to pay for your purchase if you don't have the money, and their credit rating may be affected if you don't pay on time.

MAKING PURCHASES

There's one more step before you make a major purchase: Do your research. You'll actually want to do two types of research. First, research the items or services themselves, comparing features, customer support, reliability, cost, and anything else you consider important. Second, look at reviewers' comments. Check the product and the reputation of the producer through the consumer publications and websites, such as *Consumer Reports*. Then, look at the reviews of the product and the producer in publications and on websites for the type of product. If you're purchasing a new computer, for example, look in computer magazines and on websites dedicated to high technology. You may also want to check user blogs to find out what users think about the product and whether they're having any trouble with it or with the producer or the store where they purchased it.

This research is *comparison shopping* – comparing different products, services, companies, and stores to find out what's best for you. Comparison shopping is actually educating yourself about a type of product and its market. When you educate yourself about products and producers and about the types of deals and terms you could face, you improve your chances of getting exactly what you want at a price you can afford.

Purchasing Telephone and Internet Services

A long time ago, purchasing telephone service was so easy. There was one company in a territory, and if you wanted telephone service, you went to that company. Today, the telephone industry has been deregulated, and many companies can provide many types of service in the same area. As a consumer, you have many companies to choose from.

Landline Telephone Service. Let's start with telephone service. First you must decide if you want a landline, which is a telephone connected to the service provider through connections in your home.

Your parents probably provide you with the landline telephone in your home. That landline phone can work with either a hardwired telephone connected to the wall or with a cordless phone that you can carry around when you talk. A number of telephones in the home can use the same telephone number and services. You can make local and long distance calls and can purchase a variety of options with that service, such as call waiting and voicemail. You can get landline services through a traditional phone company, such as AT&T or Verizon.

Computer-based Telephone Service. You can now get your telephone service through your computer and computer service provider. Given developments in the communications industries, this provider could be the same company that provides your landline service or it could be your Internet service provider or a cable television or satellite television provider. Because there are so many possible service providers you have more options to choose from. Advantages for purchasing computer-based telephone service can be as simple as getting a discount by including your long distance calls with your regular monthly service charge. Disadvantages can include the quality of the service; sometimes computer-based telephone calls have poor quality (static and background noise that make it difficult for all parties to hear). Another disadvantage is that, if your computer or electrical service is out, you will not be able to make calls until your service is restored.

Cell Telephone. Another option may be to use a cell telephone. Cell telephones have many advantages, including having a telephone with you when you need one (the ease and convenience) and being reachable when people need to talk with you.

Usually cell telephone packages include a number of services and options, including call waiting, voicemail, and long distance service, at no additional cost. You may also be able to send and receive text messages, take photographs, access the Internet and email, and play music on your cell telephone.

The disadvantages of using a cell telephone include:

- Losing the telephone; since you are carrying the telephone around with you, you could easily leave it behind, misplace it or damage it, or it could be stolen. It may be expensive to replace a cell telephone in the middle of your service contract. My husband dropped his phone into the snow, without realizing it. When he noticed it was missing, he retraced his steps and found

it. The screen had been damaged, and we needed to pay to have it repaired, because we were still under our contract.
- You may not be able to get cell telephone coverage in the areas in which you need the service. Here in Connecticut, I know there are certain spots where I cannot make or receive a call, or an important call may be dropped.
- You may be limited by the terms of your service contract. For example, if your plan limits you to a certain number of minutes per month, the cost of additional minutes can be expensive. Make sure you investigate each plan to find out what the per minute costs are.
- If you make calls to a location outside your plan's coverage area, you may have to pay the roaming charges, which can add up quickly.

Some people are considering not having a landline at all and using only cell telephones. When making this decision, you have to consider the advantages and disadvantages of each type of service, looking at how you use the telephone and making sure that you can get all the services you need if you use only one type of telephone.

For example, if you only have cell telephone service, what happens if you lose your telephone? You may have no telephone service at all, until you replace your telephone.

Shopping for Telephone Service. As you shop for telephone service, first decide which type of service is best for you. Then consider the advantages and disadvantages of all companies that provide service in your area and compare the prices they charge. For home telephone service, ask yourself: How much will I use the telephone? Where will I be calling – local area or long distance? Look at all types of plans with each type of company before making a decision.

CASH, CREDIT, AND YOUR FINANCES: THE TEEN YEARS

There is no reason not to tell one company what another one is offering to see if the first company can match a good deal. Sometimes these telephone service providers will compete for your business. You may decide that you need only one type of service or that you need additional features or terms. Talk to several companies to find out if they can meet your needs at a good price. Educating yourself is the best way to make choices so that you understand what you are purchasing and the possible costs associated with the choice. Don't let any company persuade you to make a choice that is not right for you and your situation.

Make sure you understand the terms of the deal (the contract) with the telephone service provider you choose. Having a contract will guarantee that you get the services you asked for at the price you agreed to for the length of the contract. The downside is that there could be substantial financial penalties if you want to make changes to the contract during its term. For example, if you have a standard two-year contract with your cell telephone company, but want to change companies mid-contract, you may have to pay as much as $175.00 as an early termination fee. So read your contract and understand what you are signing.

Bundled Services. Many service providers are bundling services. For example, your cable television service provider may also offer you Internet service and cell telephone service in one package. This bundling of services can be advantageous for you, since you'll typically receive a large discount. But be careful. Look at all the details when bundling services. How long is the price set for? What happens if you want to change companies mid-way through the contract period? Weight the discounted costs against the advantages and disadvantages for your lifestyle and needs.

Purchasing High Technology Products

It seems like every day new high technology products come onto the market, with new features and capabilities. At the same time, the computer you bought yesterday might almost seem to be obsolete today. When you are purchasing high technology products, it is essential to do your research and comparison shopping so you can make good decisions about what to buy.

Here are some questions you should ask yourself when you start to shop for a high technology product:

1. What am I looking for in this product? What do I want this product to do? How will I use it?
2. What features do I want?
3. Do I want a product from a specific manufacturer, or do I want a product with the most functionality?
4. What services do I want or need, along with this product? Can I get them with the specific products I'm looking at?
5. What else do I have to buy to make this product work? Software? Internet-based services? Auxiliaries? How much do these cost?
6. Do I want a product that works with my other high technology products? For example, do I want to be able to download files from one product to another?
7. What customer service and support do I need with this product?

When you've answered these questions, you can really start to do your research and comparison shopping. You may find yourself changing your answers to some of these questions when you find out more about the market and about what you can afford.

Important Tip: You may want to get the same brand name product a friend has, but remember that the friend's product may not meet your needs. Another friend may have the latest and hottest product, but this product may not have the functionality you want. You are the one who will be using your own product, and you must make sure that it's right for you.

....

High technology products can be purchased in stores or over the Internet. (See 'Purchasing Over the Internet,' below.) You may be able to get better price deals over the Internet, but you should weigh this against your need for service and support. Price may not be the most important factor in your decision.

Jenna just knew she had to get the iPod Nano. Jenna thought it was really cool; besides, that's what all of her friends had. After reading this chapter, though, Jenna decided to do her comparison shopping. Jenna compared the features of the iPod Nano to those of other products. She looked at ease of use, appearance, services, and compatibility. She compared prices and vendors. In the end, Jenna decided to go ahead and purchase the iPod Nano, but she was glad she had done her research. She now knew about all of the features and options and could actually show her friends neat new things they could do with their iPods.

Purchasing Your Own Car
Much of the time, people buy their first car from someone they or their families know. The transaction is friendly, with you and the other person agreeing to the terms, including the price of the car, how the payment will be handled, the condition of the car, and so forth.

If you're purchasing a car from a friend or relative, you may not have much say in the type of car and features. If you're shopping for a car, though, you can look for one that you want and that meets your needs. Some things to consider are: gas mileage, safety features, maintenance requirements, the weather and road conditions in your area, how you'll be using the car (for example, will you be hauling a boat trailer?), whether you'll be taking only local trips or whether you'll be driving across country, how long you intend to keep the car, and whether you want a new or used car. After you think about what type of car would work for you, you can start doing your research and comparison shopping.

Once you find a car that you are interested in purchasing, I suggest you follow this process. First, go online to check out the value of the car; the industry standard is the Kelley Blue Book (www.kbb.com), which is often referred to as 'the blue book.' Then you will know if the sales price is fair. If you decide to proceed, you should have a licensed mechanic examine the car to see what condition it's in. Does it need to have work done? If so, how much will that cost you? Now that you have this information, you will be able to determine what you are willing to pay for the car.

Let's assume that you are willing to purchase the car. Now the negotiations start. The seller wants to sell the car for $4,000 and you want to purchase the car. Through your research, you have found that the car is worth the $4,000, but the car needs four new tires. So you tell the seller that you are willing to purchase the car for $3,600 since you will have to replace the tires. The seller may then name another price. And you respond to that price. You and the seller will be negotiating about the price until the two of you reach an agreement.

Remember what I said in the section 'About Contracts' You will want to have the final agreement in writing, with all of the terms that you both agreed to set out, and the contract should be signed by both parties. If you are under the legal age in your state, a parent must sign for you; if you are over the legal age, you can sign the agreement.

Perhaps you have been saving your money and have enough to pay for the car you've chosen (see 'Budgeting' in Chapter 1). If you do not have the money, and if a relative is not giving you the money (see 'Borrowing from or Lending to a Friend' in Chapter 3), you will have to borrow the money through a car loan. You can do this with a bank or credit union. If you are purchasing a car from a car dealership, you could have the additional option of getting financing from the car dealership. You should be doing comparison shopping for the financing, as well as for the car itself, to get the best terms for the car loan.

Once you have been approved for the financing, you will start the steps to have the car in your name. You will need to get car insurance, either on your parent's policy or on a policy of your own. (See 'Insurance,' below) Then you will need to go to your state's Motor Vehicle Department to get the car registered in your name – if you have reached your state's legal age, typically 18 – or in your parents' or other adults' names. Now you will be the legal owner of the car.

Purchasing Over the Internet

Purchasing over the Internet is great and convenient. You know the advantages of making your purchases from your home, instead of taking the time and physical effort to go to a store. The downside is that, if you need something right away, you have to wait for the purchase to be shipped before you receive it, or you end up paying for overnight shipping, which can be costly.

There are a few things that you need to remember about doing transactions on the Internet. First, make sure that the website you are shopping on is really the vendor's official site. That's easy if you are shopping at the websites of big, well-known companies. Always type in the website address yourself, or get it from your favorites list. There is a possibility that, if you click on a link from an email message, you will not be taken to the official site. There are people out there who will try to fool you to capture your information (name, address, credit card number) for their personal and illegal uses.

For other types of websites, ones for vendors you may not know or ones representing other sellers, it becomes more difficult. Anyone can say anything on the Internet, and it's up to you to make sure that what you are purchasing is what you get. You will always want to check the return policy of the website and know what is possible for you to do and not do. Check out and understand any warranty that comes with the product you purchased. If you receive something that is not what you thought it would be, can you return it for a full refund? If something works, but stops working shortly after you buy, is there a warranty to fix the item? Most big-name companies will have this policy clearly stated on their websites.

Years ago, I wanted to purchase some electronics, and I was checking websites and stores' sale flyers. I found out something very interesting about gray market products. Gray market products are products (in my case electronics) that are substantially cheaper in price, but they are not sold through authorized distribution markets. Therefore, they are not covered by the manufacturer's warranty. Be very careful about purchasing gray market products.

When you have decided to make the purchase, here's what you should know. Never enter your information on a website that is not secure. Always look for 'https' on the URL line. The 's' stands for 'secure;' when you see it, you'll know the website is safer than an unsecured website.

Important Tip: Never send your credit card information through an email message to someone; never give out credit card information to someone who calls you, unless you really know that person.

If someone calls you and asks you to verify your information, and you did not initiate the call, ask for their name and number. Then look up the company's telephone number, call that number, and ask for the person you were speaking to. You read stories all the time in which someone was called and asked for their personal information, and only later did they find out that the call was a scam. I recently opened a bank account online, and the bank called to ask for my driver's license number. I didn't know who was calling, so I told the caller that I would be happy to bring my license to the bank the next time I was in the branch. I have no idea if this was the bank calling or someone trying to scam me. Don't be caught by such a scam.

Important Tip: Be cautious. People who are legitimate will understand why you are being cautious.

If you are shopping on an auction site, such as eBay, be especially cautious. There have been many cases in which sellers have misrepresented the products they're selling or tried to scam buyers. Make sure you use the tools available on these sites to investigate the sellers, protect yourself, and make complaints.

WARRANTIES

A *warranty*, offered by the manufacturer of a product, will guarantee all or part of your purchase for a certain amount of time from defects and for repairs that may be needed. If something that is covered by the warranty breaks or goes wrong during the set time period, the manufacturer will provide the services set out in the warranty at no cost to you.

Here's an example of something that happened to me: I purchased a color laser printer online, which came with a one-year warranty. Within one month, the printer had a problem, and the company sent a repair technician to my office to fix the printer. The technician determined that a part was needed, and he ordered the part. Our arrangement was that, as soon as I received the part, I would call the technician, who would come to install it, at no cost to me because of the warranty. I received the part, and the technician installed it. Two months later, the printer had the same problem. Again, the technician came and installed a replacement part. A few months later, the printer had the same problem. I had the same problem with my purchase three times in less than six months.

Because I had kept detailed notes that included dates, the names of people I spoke with, and the actions that took place, I was able to get the company to send me a new printer at no charge. This is the value of a warranty.

Make sure you keep and organize the paperwork for all of your purchases, along with your original sales receipts, so you can find your documentation when you need it (see 'Financial Recordkeeping,' in Chapter 1). I suggest that you staple your original sales receipt to the product manual, so it will be easily accessible when you need it.

Important Tip: If you have to waste a day or more to find the sales receipt and the contact information, you may be a day too late for your warranty to still be effective. Get in the habit of being organized. Don't procrastinate; make the call as soon as possible and keep accurate notes of who you contacted and what was said in the conversation.

Do You Need an Extended Warranty? When you purchase some products, you will be asked if you want to purchase an extended warranty. This is a warranty that will extend the set time period of the standard warranty. If the product normally comes with a one-year warranty, you may be offered the opportunity to purchase an additional two years (for a total of three years) at an additional cost. Again, you have to look at the advantages and disadvantages of the extended warranty and determine whether it is right for you.

Some people automatically buy extended warranties without even thinking about it, while others don't. For the specific product you're buying, you'll have to think about:

- How long you expect to keep this product before replacing it
- The upfront costs of the extended warranty against the possible cost of repairs
- The cost of the product itself
- The reputation of the manufacturer

Only after you think about these points can you decide whether to purchase the extended warranty. You may decide to buy the extended warranty for some products, but not for others.

INSURANCE

For most of you, the only type of insurance you will have to think about will be automobile insurance. All cars are required by their individual states to have insurance coverage. When you first get your driver's license, your parent(s) will usually add your name to their existing automobile insurance policy. That means that you will be covered in case of an accident.

When you get a car of your own (registered in your own name), you will need your own automobile insurance policy. The owner of the car is the same person who carries the insurance policy. Each state has its own requirements, minimum dollar amounts, and terms for what insurance you must purchase. The types of coverage you will likely need are:

- Liability, which includes bodily injury and property damage
- Medical payments, for injuries from an accident

- Uninsured /underinsured motorist, which includes bodily injury
- Damage to your automobile (other than collision). For example, a severe storm could knock over a tree that falls onto your car.

Other insurance options are available to you, including:

- Damage to your auto (collision). Collision is the coverage that you need for your own car if you are at fault in the accident. Some people don't carry collision coverage if they are driving an older car because the value of their car is low and they would not fix the car if they were in an accident. They would replace it instead. As your car gets older, it costs more for collision coverage, so you need to decide when it's not worth the cost.
- Glass coverage. This doesn't cost much, and it could be good to have. If you are driving on the highway and the car in front of you kicks up a rock that cracks your windshield, you would be covered.
- Rental car coverage. If your car cannot be driven after an accident, you may need to rent a vehicle. This coverage could cover the cost of the rental car while yours is being fixed.

If you are in an accident, you should notify your insurance company, and they will start the process. Your insurer will determine whose fault the accident is. If it is your fault, you will be covered, minus your deductible amount. If the other person is at fault, your insurance company will ask the other person's insurance company to reimburse them for the money that they gave to you. If the driver at fault doesn't have enough coverage, your uninsured/underinsured motorist coverage kicks in. You can both be found to be at fault – perhaps you're considered 40% at fault and the other driver 60% at fault – and your insurance coverage will be adjusted.

When you are shopping for automobile insurance, you may deal with one of two basic types of insurance companies. The first type is a *direct company*; an agent may represent only one insurance company or you deal with the company directly via telephone or its website. The other type of insurance company represents multiple insurance companies; you could go to one insurance agent and get rate quotes from multiple insurance companies. These types of companies are called *brokerages*.

Insurance can be very expensive, so you will want to do as much as possible to keep your costs as low as possible. You will want to do comparison shopping for both policy terms and prices. Some companies offer discounts for getting good grades or successfully completing a driver's education class. You may also get discounts for having safety features in the car, such as antilock brakes, air bags, and anti-theft devices. Check to see if you qualify for any types of discounts because of affinities or memberships in certain organizations.
The type of automobile you drive can affect your insurance costs, too. That brand new sports car will cost more to insure than the economy car that's several years old.

Summary:
To protect yourself when you make a major purchase, you should have the terms of the purchase set out in a written contract.

Before you make a major purchase, you should research the product itself and do comparison shopping. You can find information in consumer publications, product publications, websites about the product, and users' blogs.

Be alert when you are making major purchases. Make sure the products you are considering meet your specific needs and are affordable. Beware of scams, particularly when shopping over the Internet. Make sure that you are getting what you paid for, know how to get customer support and service for the product, and are making good decisions about warranties and insurance.

To get your **Implementation Checklist & Resources Guide**s, please go to **www. YourFinances.com/Guides** to download your free copies.

AFTERWORD:
WHAT THE TEENAGERS LEARNED

I gave each of the teenagers a copy of this book, and most of them read it and used the information in it to help them plan for their finances.

Sally had already learned the value of savings most of her wages. She was very interested to learn that different banks and different types of accounts could pay her higher rates of interest, so she did some research and switched her savings account. Sally plans to go on to college – that's why she saving – but she became aware that she wouldn't be able to save enough just through her jobs. She started researching funding options and contacting government agencies and schools for more information. Two years from now, when Sally is applying to colleges, she'll be prepared and ready to act.

Greg has discovered the value of planning for his financial future. He used his computer skills to set up Quicken and has set a budget and organized his finances. He figured out that, if he takes on more projects to make more money, he may even be able to do a little investing. Greg loves doing research on his computer, and he's found a number of websites that will educate him about investing options. He's also gone to websites for information about paying for his education, He's hoping for a merit scholarship, but realizes that he'll need more money than that and his savings to cover his expenses.

Scott used the information to help search for college funding. He also started setting a budget for himself, matching his income against expenses. Before, he had just sort of been aware of these numbers, but he's learned how important it is to keep good records. Most important, Scott has gotten real about how much money he'll need over the coming years and about how much (or little, actually) he's be able to spend.

Jenna's parents had been teaching her to be responsible about savings and working, The most important thing she learned was the value of making purchases wisely. She has a lot of fun doing her comparison shopping and felt that she was learning how to become a responsible consumer. Jenna has set a new goal: Earning enough to make a down payment on a car by her 16th birthday. She has already started comparing types of cars and deals and has talked with her parents about driver's education and insurance.

Sally, Greg, Scott and Jenna are learning to manage their money well. They have picked up the basic concepts in the book, and they are using the information as it applies to their lives. I'm sure that they will develop solid financial futures for themselves.

Peter took his copy of the book and threw it in the corner of his room, where it was quickly covered by magazines and clothing. Meanwhile, he's been unsuccessful in getting a new credit card, he's wondering why some of his friends have stopped lending him money, and his parents are hinting that they won't help him pay for college unless he becomes more responsible about money.

I hope I've persuaded you to become like Sally, Greg Scott and Jenna and start to assume responsibility for your own finances and future. As for Peter – well, what do you think will happen to him?

GLOSSARY

Average daily balance method A method of calculating the interest due on a credit card balance by multiplying the interest rate by the amount owed every day

Bank check A check issued by a bank, which draws on funds you give the bank or have on deposit

Budget A plan for managing your money which tracks both income and spending in various categories

Cashiers' check A type of bank check drawn against money you have on deposit

Certificate of Deposit A form of savings account in which someone deposits a sum of money for a set period of time, while getting a higher rate of interest

Certified check A personal check that has been guaranteed by a bank against money on deposit

Checking account An account, usually based in banks, that allows the depositor to write checks against an already-deposited sum of money

Commercial bank A type of bank established to serve and meet the needs of businesses

Comparison shopping Educating oneself about products and markets by looking at different products, services, companies, and vendors

Contract An agreement between two parties, containing the names and signatures of the parties, the details of the terms, and the date

Credit The privilege offered to you by a bank, financial institution, or store of purchasing now, but paying later

Credit card A non-cash means of payment for purchases extended to individuals who qualify based on history of managing credit and debt

Credit limit The maximum dollar amount you can draw upon from any one lender

Credit report A summation of your use of credit and debt and your record of paying bills, maintained by the three credit reporting agencies
Credit reporting agencies The three agencies (Equifax, Experian, and TransUnion) responsible for creating, monitoring, and distributing credit reports
Credit score A three-digit number that reflects a person's credit-worthiness
Credit union A type of financial institution formed to provide many banking services to members of a common group
Debit Card A type of bank card that withdraws funds from a checking account when used to make a purchase
Direct deposit A form of electronic banking, in which an employer deposits a paycheck directly into an employee's account
Electronic banking A catch-all term that covers services offered by banks that can be conducted over the Internet
Electronic funds transfer (ETF) A form of electronic banking in which a checking account holder transfers money to another entity or person, without writing a check
Estimated taxes Quarterly payments to the federal and state governments to cover anticipated income taxes due on April 15 of the subsequent year; see 'Withholding taxes'
Expenses The costs of purchasing products and services
Federal Deposit Insurance Company (FDIC) A federal agency that insures your deposits in a bank up to a certain amount
Federal Reserve System The federal entity that oversees the US banking system and manages the money supply
Free Application for Federal Student Aid (FAFSA) A form to be filled out by a student, which serves as the starting point for educational loans from the federal government
Grace period The time between the use of credit or the receiving of a loan and the date the first repayment is due
Gross wages The amount of money you earned at a job, before deductions are made

Identity theft The use of someone else's personal information for illegal purposes
Income Money received from various sources, including salaries and wages, gifts, interest, and investments
Income tax Annual payments due to federal, state, and sometimes local governments based on money received during the year; see 'Estimated taxes' and 'Withholding taxes'
Insurance A contract between an insurer and the insured to provide compensation for defined people, products, or services in case of defined accidents, damage, or other problems
Investment accounts Deposits of money in investments (such as stock or bonds) or retirement savings (such as IRAs, 401K plans, and similar options)
Internet/virtual bank A type of bank that provides basic banking services solely over the Internet
Loan An amount borrowed from a financial institution, which must be repaid
Money market account An account, usually based in a bank, which is used to save money, while providing the ability to write checks
Money order A type of bank check written by the bank for the amount of money you give the bank
National Credit Union Share Insurance Fund (NCSIF) A federal agency that insures your deposits in a credit union up to a certain amount
Parent loan A loan to cover educational expenses, taken out in the parents' names
Principal The amount of a loan
Property taxes Payments to state and local governments based on owning certain property, such as a car or a boat
Register A log in which you can keep track of activity in a checking account or other financial account
Safe deposit box A repository, usually located in a bank or other financial institution, for keeping important papers and possessions

Sales tax Payments to state and sometimes local governments based on the value of items you purchase
Savings Money put aside for investment or future purchases
Savings account An account, usually based in a bank, used to accumulate money on which interest is paid
Savings & Loan A type of bank established to meet the needs of individuals
Scholarship Money extended by schools and organizations to help pay for an education, with no expectation or requirement of being repaid
Secured credit Credit that is extended based on the value of an item to support the loan
Social Security A federal government program, under which money deducted from a person's income is credited to that person's account, for use in retirement
Student loan A loan to cover educational expenses, taken out in the student's name
Student Loan Marketing Association (Sallie Mae) A company that provides education loans, information, and consolidation loans to support students and their families in paying educational expenses
Subsidized loan A type of student loan under which the federal government pays the interest due while the student is in school
Travelers' check A check issued by a financial institution which can be replaced if lost or stolen
Two-cycle billing average method A method of calculating the interest on a credit card balance by multiplying the interest rate by the average amount owed over two billing cycles
Universal default A status under which a borrower, who has made a late payment on a bill, finds it difficult to get more credit and has interest rates on credit cards increase
Unsecured credit Credit that is granted without being supported by assets or items of value
Unsubsidized loan A type of student loan on which the student pays interest to the lender

Warranty A guarantee by a manufacturer of a product to cover the costs of repair and replacement of defective parts for a set period of time

Withholding taxes Deductions from paychecks and sent to the federal and state governments to cover anticipated income tax due on April 15 of the subsequent year; see 'Estimated taxes'

Work/study program A way of paying for an education under which the student works at an on-campus job and gets credit toward education costs

INDEX

A

Allowance · 3, 6, 8, 16, 17, 18, 20, 25

B

Banks · 17, 24, 27, 28, 29, 30, 31, 32, 34, 35, 36, 37, 38, 40, 41, 48, 51, 70, 77, 81, 109
  Accounts · 17, 23, 30, 32, 36, 37, 38, 48, 101
  Checks · 2, 28, 35, 36, 39, 42, 43, 44, 45, 46, 47
  Commercial · 27, 28, 29, 33, 48, 51, 111
  Fees · 38
  Internet/Virtual · 27, 29, 33, 113
  Savings & Loan · 28, 29, 31, 33, 48, 51, 82, 114
  Selecting · 40
  Services · 36, 48, 49, 51
Budget · 6, 7, 9, 10, 11, 15, 25, 50, 58, 67, 109, 111

C

Certificates of Deposit · 36, 111
Checking Accounts · 6, 7, 32, 34, 35, 36, 38, 39, 41, 42, 43, 45, 48, 50, 111
  Balancing · 47
  Bounced Checks · 39
  Check 21 Rule · 49
  Deposits · 43, 45, 47
  Fees · 38
  Opening · 41
  Register · 44, 113
  Writing Checks · 43
Contracts · 83, 84, 89, 90, 99, 111
Credit · 1, 3, 4, 6, 22, 24, 27, 53, 54, 55, 59, 62, 63, 65, 66, 67, 70, 76, 79, 82, 87, 111, 112, 113, 114
  Establishing · 53, 54, 55, 56, 57, 66, 70, 89
  Maintaining · 65, 85, 87, 88
  Report · 54, 55, 62, 63, 64, 65, 112
  Reporting Agencies · 55, 58, 61, 62, 63, 64, 112
  Score · 54, 55, 62, 64, 65, 66, 68, 70, 75, 81, 87, 88, 91, 112
Credit Cards · 1, 23, 32, 53, 54, 57, 58, 59, 60, 61, 65, 66, 67, 68, 70, 110, 111
  Fees · 59, 60, 67, 70
  Terms · 56, 58, 59, 60
  Types · 55, 57
Credit Union · 27, 31, 34, 36, 51, 81, 99, 112

D

Debt · 1, 9, 10, 53, 54, 61, 66, 67, 68, 70, 78, 89
  Managing · 66, 68
  Paying Down · 67

E

Education · 1, 5, 6, 7, 17, 71, 72, 73, 74, 76, 77, 79, 80, 81, 82, 83, 84, 87, 88, 106, 109, 110
Expenses · 71, 72

Paying for · 72, 73, 74, 76, 77, 81
Electronic Banking · 29, 34, 39, 48, 49, 51, 53, 112
Expenses · 6, 7, 8, 9, 10, 16, 17, 35, 76, 82, 109

F

Federal Reserve System · 27, 28, 112
Financial Aid · 72, 76, 81, 84, 85, 86, 88

I

Identity Theft · 23, 24, 64, 113
Income · 2, 8, 10, 14, 17, 20, 61, 73, 75, 76, 109, 113
Insurance · 13, 21, 22, 87, 99, 104, 105, 106, 107, 110, 113
Investing · 6, 109

L

Loans · 9, 27, 28, 36, 54, 70, 72, 74, 75, 76, 77, 78, 80, 81, 82, 83, 84, 85, 86, 87, 88, 113, 114
   Car · 9, 55, 64, 66, 99
   Federal Government · 80, 85
   Parent · 75
   Paying back · 87
   Private · 75, 81
   Qualifying for · 84
   State government · 78
   Student · 77, 114
   Terms · 83

M

Money · 1, 2, 3, 4, 5, 6, 7, 8, 9, 10, 15, 16, 17, 18, 19, 20, 21, 25, 28, 32, 34, 35, 36, 38, 39, 41, 42, 44, 45, 46, 47, 49, 50, 54, 56, 59, 65, 67, 68, 69, 70, 72, 73, 74, 75, 81, 82, 83, 85, 87, 89, 91, 99, 105, 109, 110, 111, 114
Money Market Accounts · 35, 113

P

Paycheck · 3, 12, 14, 15, 17, 20, 21, 38, 39, 41, 48, 87, 112
   Deductions · 20, 21, 22
   Handling · 20
Purchases · 6, 12, 18, 23, 25, 32, 37, 54, 57, 58, 59, 68, 89, 100, 103, 107, 110, 114
   Car · 98, 99
   High Technology Products · 96, 97
   Over the Internet · 100
   Telephone and Internet Services · 92, 93, 94, 95

R

Recordkeeping · 11

S

Safe Deposit Box · 13, 36, 37, 113
Savings · 1, 3, 7, 9, 10, 16, 17, 18, 19, 21, 25, 27, 28, 33, 35, 36, 38, 41, 50, 51, 56, 72, 73, 76, 77, 109, 110, 114

Savings Accounts · 2, 6, 14, 16, 17, 32, 34, 35, 51, 114
  Deposits · 35, 42
  Opening · 35, 41
Scholarships · 72, 74, 78, 79, 81, 82, 86, 88, 114
  Qualifying for · 84
  Types of · 74
Social Security · 20, 21, 22, 23, 41, 43, 114
Student Loan Marketing Association (Sallie Mae) · 71, 78, 114

T

Tax Returns · 14, 16
Taxes · 2, 3, 14, 15, 16, 18, 20, 73
  Estimated · 15, 112, 113
  Income · 14, 15, 21, 22, 112, 113, 115
  Property · 15, 113
  Sales · 15, 114
  Withholding · 15, 21, 113, 115

W

Warranties · 12, 104, 107, 115
Websites
  Author's · 4, 6, 19, 25, 51, 70, 72, 88, 107
  Consumer · 62, 98
  Government · 24
  Managing Money · 40
  Paying for Education · 71, 78
Work/Study Program · 73, 76, 77, 81, 86, 115

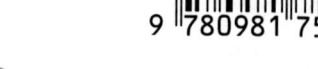